CHALLENGES ACCEPTED

Twenty-Four Hours to Live?

JIM CECIL

PAGE PUBLISHING, INC.
Conneaut Lake, PA

First originally published by Page Publishing 2019

ISBN 978-1-64584-305-4 (pbk)
ISBN 978-1-64701-270-0 (hc)
ISBN 978-1-64584-306-1 (digital)

Printed in the United States of America

To Mark Novak and the Lake Monticello Fire and Rescue Squads.

CONTENTS

FOREWORD

When I was about five years old, my family—my mother, my siblings, and I—were forced to leave our home in Roanoke City.

For years, I had no clue as to why, but I still remember the scene quite well.

Huddled together in one of the bedrooms upstairs in our split-level home on Frontier Road, we peered out one of the windows on a cold winter day in anticipation of our maternal grandfather, Ezra Munsey, pulling up in his old blue-and-white Buick Special, to gather us and take us to his and his wife's home in nearby Salem. When he exited the vehicle and approached our door, I noticed that he had a tear in his eye.

I asked my mother, "Why is Granddaddy crying?"

She said, "I don't know."

Suddenly my mother began to cry, and I felt confused.

Ezra, approximately sixty-four at the time, was about to serve in the role as a father again since ours had abandoned us.

He and Mary Smith Munsey had been married for many years and had two children—including a son who was still living in the home.

Fourteen years older than I, Galen Munsey was nineteen when we moved in the Munsey home and began what must have felt to them like a huge encroachment.

Surely our mere presence—a mother and her four small children—was quite the imposition on Galen and his parents, but we were family, so they took us in.

One of the things that I will always remember about Galen was that he had nice friends. Soon after moving into our new home, I met one of those friends.

I recall that he and I were sitting on the couch in the living room. He was a big man, and he was wearing his Andrew Lewis High School football jersey. I still remember that the number on the jersey was 72.

He was gentle and very playful. He laughed when he lifted me into the air.

His name was Jimmy Cecil.

After that happy and playful time, I don't recall ever seeing him again.

That is, not until more than fifty years later.

Our reunification, of sorts, was prompted by the publishing of my third book, *The Team the Titans Remember*, which came out in October 2017.

In the acknowledgments section, I included Galen Munsey at the top of the list because he was the person who took me to see many of the Andrew Lewis High "Wolverines" Football Team's games. Had he not done so, my emotional and personal connection to the team would have been questionable, or possibly even nonexistent. And if I had not written the book, Jimmy Cecil and I might have never reconnected.

For the record, Galen is an alumnus of Andrew Lewis, class of 1961, and so is Jimmy Cecil, class of 1960.

When Jimmy learned of the book and read of Galen Munsey, he reached out to me via e-mail and introduced himself as a friend of Galen's.

Though he didn't remember having met me when I was a child, I told him that I certainly remembered having met him.

We immediately connected and began socializing. At our first meeting, we had lunch in Charlottesville, Virginia, where I autographed a copy of my book and presented him with a commemorative hat courtesy of former Andrew Lewis assistant coach Dale Foster.

Soon afterward, he told me of his desire to publish an autobiography. He asked for my assistance in plowing through the publication process. Eventually, he asked me to write the foreword for his book which, of course, I was honored to do.

What is striking about his story is this: For a man who has endured much—including a dysfunctional family past and a myriad of health problems and hospitalizations—he is amazingly still a gentle, thoughtful, and kind person. When you read his story, you may be amazed to learn that he never became jaded, cynical, or even angry as many of us may have become if similarly situated.

He obviously made the conscious decision early on in his life to make the most of every situation and not let negative events shape his thinking or outlook on life.

You will be amazed at the extreme level of adversity he has overcome. Suffice it to say that many of us might have given up on life had we been confronted with similar setbacks.

His story begins with a sad remembrance of an event that happened during his childhood. Tragically, his father literally rode right out of his life.

He did so at a time when posttraumatic stress disorder had not yet been discovered. That, coupled with alcohol abuse, helps explain this man's erratic—and sometimes cruel—behavior. Jimmy's mother soon suffered a nervous breakdown after her husband abandoned her and their two children. It was too much for her to handle, and she was committed to a mental institution. Jimmy and his only sibling, an older brother named Billy, were now orphans.

While it may be tempting at times for the reader to feel sad, Jimmy Cecil continually found the resolve to not only overcome adversity, but to also pursue his dreams and make them realities. One of those recent dreams was to write a book, and yet there's nothing self-serving about his story. He didn't write his book to become wealthy or see it become a best seller.

He wrote it to inspire others.

I know it has inspired me.

And I trust that it will inspire you.

—Mark A. O'Connell
Author of *The Team the Titans Remember* and
Criminal Minds in Real Time and *Justice Denied*

A GLORIOUS CELEBRATION

Tuesday, May 8, 1945
My Grandparents' home, Johnson City, Tennessee

I jumped out of bed in anticipation of a really fun day. Mom had promised to take my older brother, Billy, and I to a park for a picnic lunch. We would then stay long enough to feed the squirrels and the birds. If there was still time, we might get to go to the movies. I was only three years old, and I didn't understand a lot of things.

For example, when I asked my mom why our dad did not live with us, she said that he was away in a strange land called Europe.

She explained, "He is in a terrible place where he has to fight mean people that are trying to hurt him. He is brave, and you should be proud of him." One time she told us he had been hurt and was in a hospital, and I cried. One day long after that, she said he was going to be all right.

"Is he going to come home to live with us?" we asked.

She sadly answered, "Yes, but it will not be anytime soon."

It turned out to be a beautiful day, and I hurriedly sprinted in to the living room to hug Mom. She was bent over the radio, almost in a trance. Before she could rise, I hit her with a big hug, yelling, "This is going to be the best day of my life!"

She surprised me when she responded, "Yes, and maybe for our whole family." She went on to say, "We may not be able to go on our picnic today. There is something important that I must hear on the radio. I promise to make it up to you guys."

Before I could get cranked up for one of my best "crying tantrums," she apparently heard what was so important. She grabbed the radio, pulling the plug out of the wall socket. In the same motion she screamed, "It is over, it is over, he can come home, he is coming home!"

All of a sudden car horns were blowing out on the street and church bells were ringing. Billy joined us, and we followed her out the front door. There were crowds of people dancing around and yelling in the middle of the streets. Mom joined them, and Billy and I sat on the steps of the porch and watched. It seemed to us that the whole world had gone crazy. The celebrating and craziness went on for weeks thereafter. It was all that our neighbors and friends talked about or even cared about.

As I reminisce about these strange events in my young life, I now know the fighting that my mom had told me about was World War II, and my dad was in the Army. Of course, May 8, 1945, was VE Day (Victory in Europe), the day that Germany surrendered to the Allied Forces.

Later, after another enemy, Japan, also surrendered, the war was officially over. It meant peace (at least for a while) and that our soldiers would be coming home. It took a long time for all our troops to deploy from their duties. It was almost two years later that our dad received his honorable discharge and returned to us. I was now five years old, and it was exciting to finally learn what it meant to have both my parents. Unfortunately, for my family, it did not turn out well at all.

DAD COMES HOME

It had been almost two years since the war in Europe ended and my dad was still over there.

My mom said, "Most of the countries were in combat zones, and the people's homes and cities were now destroyed. Since your dad is a civil engineer, it was necessary for him to stay and help with the restoration of the buildings, bridges, and roads."

However, Mom received a telegram from him a few days ago letting her know that he had completed his tour of duty and would be arriving back home that day. We were all excited to finally have our family complete. Billy and I had been discussing how great it would be to have a dad to take care of us, protect us, and always be there for us.

He was a brilliant man who had graduated from VPI (now known as Virginia Tech). After the war ended, he had a lot of time on his hands while in Europe to submit résumés and job applications to prospective employers here in the United States. He did not have much luck at first, but about a year ago, he received and accepted an offer from the Highway Department (now known as VDOT, or Virginia Department of Transportation). It was a civil engineer position in Wytheville, Virginia. They agreed to hold the position open until he came home. When my mother found out, she also looked for a job in Wytheville and was able to obtain a teaching position. Wytheville was a small friendly town located in Southwest Virginia.

She had rented a house there, and we had moved before Dad came home.

Dad arrived right on schedule, and we picked him up at the train station. Mom had organized a "welcome home" party, which included some of the neighbors and a few relatives. We were disappointed when he arrived wearing civilian clothes instead of his uniform. We made him put it on to model it for all the guests.

He patiently explained to us, "The gold oak leaf on my collar signifies my rank, major." His chest was covered with medals of many shapes and colors, including numerous combat ribbons, a Bronze Star, a Purple Heart, American Service Medal, European African Middle Eastern Service Medal, and World War II Victory Medal.

He had fought in a number of battles, including Normandy, Northern France, Ardennes, Rhineland, and Central Europe. He was wounded June 1, 1945, at Metz, France.

I noticed that after a while, he seemed to become sullen and moody. When I asked Mom, "Is Dad not happy to be home?"

She answered, "He is just tired from his long trip." Then she confessed, "He told me that he was never going to wear his uniform again and he did not want to ever talk about the war."

The next day the celebrating was over, and it was time for our family to adjust to peacefully living together.

LIVING IN WYTHEVILLE

September 1, 1947
102 Chestnut Street, Wytheville, Virginia

It had been a few months since Dad's "homecoming," and we had gone through the initial phases of getting to know each other better. It appeared to most of our friends and neighbors that we were a normal happy family. All seemed well at 102 Chestnut Street. Dad liked his job, and the Highway Department was pleased with his work. It was the beginning of a school year, and Mom was glad to be back in the classroom. Billy was a model student and was beginning the third grade. One of our neighbors stayed with me until Mom got home from school each day.

However, sometimes appearances can be deceiving.

When Dad came home as a decorated war hero, we were all proud of him. He had brought home awards, medals, and souvenirs. Among the spoils of war were a huge Nazi flag with a swastika, a German dagger, and brass knuckles. The best prize he had managed to collect were two bricks from Hitler's home, Berchtesgaden. He had them made into bookends engraved in gold with his name and rank (they now sit on my bookshelf). Unfortunately, he also brought home something else, a serious drinking habit. His addiction grew worse until he became a full-fledged alcoholic. Some "drunks" are silly and funny when they are intoxicated. When he drank, which was every night, he was mean. I was too young to understand, but I quickly learned to fear him when he became physically and mentally abusive. I soon found out what a destructive tragedy alcoholism could be. Even though I was only five years old, it was plain to me that my dad's life was going to be lived inside a bottle.

As for me, my life was a mixed bag made up of happy times and difficult situations. My brother, Billy, was now eight, and he excelled at everything he did. He was my parents' favorite, and they adored him. In the 1960s through the 1990s, there was a musical comedy duo named the "Smothers Brothers." In their act, they constantly argued as to who their parents liked the most. The younger one, Tommy, always accused Dick as being their favorite. That was the same situation in our family. Billy always got the best toys, and I was stuck with cheap ones. More often than not, I was the recipient of his worn-out clothes and playthings.

As I now remember, my life up to that point was mostly a happy one. Regardless of whatever problems arose, I always maintained a good, positive attitude. One of the things that I liked to do the most was to go to the movies on Saturday. There was always a good "western" to see, and I idolized Roy Rodgers, Gene Autry, Red Ryder and Little Beaver, the Lone Ranger, and Lash Larue. For thirty-five cents, you could see a good "flick" and have some money leftover for candy. Unlike today, you didn't arrive at the theater when the movie started. Instead you walked in during the show. Sometimes it was in the middle or right at the end. When they "reran" it back to the beginning, you simply watched what you had missed. Of course, you would eventually get to the scene where you would turn to the person you were with and say, "This is where we came in." At that point you could get up and leave or you could stay and watch the ending all over again. Back then when you went to the theater, in addition to the movie, there were two other "bonuses." One of these extras was always a cartoon. Some of the most popular ones were Bugs Bunny, Tom and Jerry, and Mighty Mouse. Also, even better than that were the "serials" that the theaters would show. These "serials" ran with a different chapter each week, and they usually were fifteen chapters long. Each "serial" featured one particular hero who would face a new death-defying situation at the end of that week's episode. At the end, right at the last second, a message would appear on the screen, "To be continued." You knew it was impossible for them to live, but they always found a way to survive. Of course, you had to come back next week to find out how. Most of these "serials" had titles like *The Desert Hawk*, *Raiders of Ghost City*, and *The Tiger Woman*. Some of the others were superheroes which are still extremely popular today. Many of them can trace their roots from comic books—for example, Batman, Captain America, and Superman. I loved watching my "western" superstars so much that I tried to emulate them by killing off the bad guys in make-believe gun battles. Other kids in the neighborhood would join in for group "shoot-outs." I still remember that all I wanted for Christmas one year was a two gun belt and holster complete with six-shooter pistols. The belt was made to hold a holster and gun on your left hip and another holster and gun on the right hip, quite a lethal arsenal. However, Dad and Mom could not find a belt that had left and right holsters. So they came up with what they thought was a unique solution. One of them said, "Why don't' we just buy two right-hand holsters." I am sure it was the kind of idea a civil engineer would come up with. Good solution, right? Not quite! When I put the belt on with the right holster and gun on the right, it was fine. However, when I put the other right hand holster on the left hip, both the holster and the gun were backward. This made it impossible to win fast-draw shoot-outs and made me the laughing stock of my playmates.

Another Christmas, Billy and I both asked for and received new bicycles. Billy got an expensive Schwinn, which was the top of the line, the Black Phantom. It had chrome fenders and a huge spring on the front which served as a shock absorber. It was absolutely beautiful. What did I get? Mine was a cheap Murray girls' bike. Looking back now, I don't think it mattered much. One day I was flying down a hill and crashed into the back of a parked car. The bicycle was totaled, and there was not much left of it that was straight. As it turned out, my dad refused to replace it. I had to put what was left of the usable parts back together to make a rideable bicycle. I accomplished the reconstruction but was stuck with a bike with no fenders. I quickly learned why bikes have fenders. Every time I rode mine, it threw mud or water up, and I got a face full. Guiding it presented another problem. The handlebars were bent, and they pointed in a direction other than the way you were heading.

I had always loved animals, and we had two dogs during our stay in Wytheville. The first one was a Boston terrier named Butch who was with us about six months. Tragically, he contracted a disease known as mange. The definition of this disease is that it causes a loss of hair on canines from mites. These mites will burrow into the skin, creating intense itching and irritation. Poor Butch was suffering and had to be put down.

Several months later, I talked Dad and Mom in to letting me have another Boston terrier, which I named Frisky. I fed him and took care of him for several months. However, when I got home from school one day, I quickly realized he was missing. He did not come home for a week, and I suspected that Dad had done something with him.

I asked Mom, "What has happened to Frisky?"

She answered, "He is gone, and he is not coming back." She sadly looked at me, and I could tell that she knew that I needed a better exclamation. She then confessed, "Your dad did not want to keep him any longer, so he took him about forty miles up in the mountains and left him there."

I was heartbroken, and I had one more reason to hate him.

Three more weeks went by when one morning I heard a noise at our back door. I investigated to see what it was, and there sat Frisky. He was dirty, tired, and skinny. He apparently had somehow retraced the trip from the mountains back to our house. Scientist have researched how dogs and cats are able to return from long trips even when they are taken there in cars or trucks. One theory is that they use magnetic earth signs. Another idea is that they rely on their keen sense of smell to retrace the route. It didn't matter to me how he did it, just that he was back. My sadness was replaced by my joy to have him in my arms again.

However, two weeks later, he disappeared again. This time Mom did not try to hide the truth. Between the tears, she told me, "Your father took Frisky up in the mountains again. He put him out of the car and set a pan of food in front of him. While the poor dog was eating, he shot him with his army .45 automatic pistol."

Eventually I got over the loss of Frisky, but I never forgot or forgave my dad.

First Grade in Wytheville

My last year of living in Wytheville was spent in the first grade. My teacher, Ms. Stevens, was a nice lady, and I enjoyed school. I was not the brightest crayon in the box, but I think part of the problem was my laziness. Toward the last month of the year, she had the class reading from some "beginner" books. We were given assignments to practice at home and then read out loud the next day. Ms. Stevens expected everyone to be able to read the same page, and she always called on us according to our last name. For each assignment she would start at the beginning of the alphabet with the letter *A*. This meant that since my name was Cecil, I would be one of the first readers. This presented a problem since I didn't bother to do my homework and had not bothered to even look at it. A quick glance at the book told me that I would not be able to read this page. It was clear to me that I must now devise an escape strategy. Maybe I could fake an illness or tell her that I had to go to the restroom. Let's see, how about if I told her my eyes have gone blurred or even better that I was temporally blind. All these seemed believable to me, but I knew she would not be convinced. Suddenly I was in "double warp speed panic mode." There was no way out, and I would have to bite the bullet and beg for mercy.

However, my prayers were answered when she announced, "Today we are going to read page 26." She continued and said, "This time we are going to begin at the end of the alphabet, and that means you, Jerry Zimmerman." So now I was thinking, *Go for it, Jerry, you are the man, Jerry.*

All of a sudden, I was brought back to reality. It dawned on me that when she got close to the beginning of the alphabet, it would be my turn. I was not off the hook yet, so it was back to the drawing board. I thought to myself, *How am I going to get out of this one?* As I pondered my predicament, the idea light flickered in my brain. *I may not be able to read, but my memory is still working,* I concluded. My plan was to carefully listen to my classmates as they read. When it finally came to my turn, I would have the entire page totally and actually memorized. It did not take long to get to the *C*s. It was show-time, and I knocked it out, never missing a beat. Ms. Stevens congratulated me after everyone took their turn and exclaimed, "Jimmy, that was very good, you were the best reader today." I felt like saying, "It was a piece of cake," but I kept my silence.

Another memory I have of being in the first grade was an embarrassing incident that occurred one day on the way to school. I had to walk to school each day, and this required me to walk several blocks down Chestnut Street to reach Main Street. After making a right onto Main Street, I had another fifteen blocks to hike through the middle of town before I reached the school. One day after I had reached the halfway point, I somehow managed to tear the seat out of my pants. This left a huge opening exposing my backside and left me with no alternative other than using one of my textbooks to cover it up. Upon arriving at school, I tried to avoid everyone and quickly occupied my desk. It was certain that I was not going to get up the rest of the day.

I was able to stay put until lunchtime when I let Ms. Stevens know, "I am on a special diet, and lunch is out of the question for me."

She then asked, "Are you on a diet because of some serious ailment?"

Without giving it much thought, I replied, "Oh yes, the doctors say I am suffering from airttickalitist."

I didn't get any response from her as she walked away. It was a good bet that before the day was over, she would try to look up airttickalitist. As soon as she left the room, I took the opportunity to use the bathroom. It rained that afternoon, so we stayed inside for recess. After school ended, the walk down Main Street awaited me. The only solution was to once again revert to the textbook-on-the-backside trick. Of course, it did not occur to me that the sight of a six-year-old boy walking down the street holding a book to his rear end created more stares than simply walking with torn pants. The next thing I had to contend with would be Mom's anger because I had ruined a good pair of slacks. However, I was at the top of my game, and I solved that problem by wrapping the pants in newspaper and depositing them in a trash can.

It really didn't matter because I found her in a state of panic, and I knew something important had happened.

She excitedly said, "Your dad received some news today, but I will wait until Billy gets home from school to tell you."

TRIP TO WARSAW

As soon as Billy showed up, Mom sat us down and told us what the big news was.

She explained, "Your father has gotten a promotion, and he has been transferred. We have to get everything packed up and be ready to go as soon as the school year ends."

"Where are we going to be living?" I asked.

"In Warsaw," she replied.

If she had said to Mars, it would have made about as much sense to me. I had no idea where or what Warsaw was. The next several weeks were hectic and disorganized to say the least. Back in those days, a lot of people did not own their homes but instead rented them from the owners. You could rent them furnished or unfurnished. Mom and Dad never owned a home, and they possessed very little furniture, which made moving easier. Also they did not have to sell our present house nor purchase another one to move into. They hired movers to haul most of our belongings, including any large items. We packed our clothes and a few small necessities in our car. We said goodbye to Wytheville and began our journey east to Warsaw. The trip reminded me of some of the westerns that I had seen at the movie theater in which the pioneer settlers had traveled west in Conestoga wagons on the Oregon Trail. We also were heading for a strange new world. The difference was, we were riding in a 1947 Ford instead of a Praire Schooner and we were not under attack by hostile Indians. The only Indians that I saw were the Pontiac cars we passed on the highway.

Warsaw was near the eastern coast of Virginia fifty-two miles east of Richmond. We had a long hot trip ahead of us. There were no interstate highways, and we were beginning a trek, which would cover over three hundred miles and would take about six hours to complete depending how many stops we made. There were no McDonalds or any other fast-food restaurants or gas stations. There were only privately owned "mom-and-pop" establishments, and those were sparse. This meant there were no bathroom or eating breaks in the travel itinerary. Looking back now, there is one word that best describes this excursion: *miserable*! Billy and I were restless, our parents argued the entire trip, and we had a small kitten with us. Its name was Itsy because we didn't know if it was a male or female. To help you create an imaginary vision of this disaster for yourself, think what it was like to be the parents of two young kids, a complaining spouse, and a cat in a 1947 Ford. Keep in mind that cars back then lacked many conveniences that are available today. Air-conditioning was not in vehicles then and was not offered until around 1953. Power steering was introduced in 1951, and power brakes not until the 1970s. The windows which were important since there was no other way to get fresh air (unless you owned a convertible) had to be raised and lowered with a hand crank located on each door. On each side of the car there was a small triangle-shaped window vent which could be opened to allow a small amount of air into the automobile.

One incident during the trip that I will never forget occurred about six miles before we reached our destination. We had reached a small town named Tappahannock. It was constructed on the banks of a major river, the Rahannock River. To cross the river, we had to drive across a long, wide bridge. We had reached the halfway point when Dad suddenly pulled over to the side and announced, "Let's get out and stretch our legs and look down at the water."

We were all glad to get out of the car to get some air. My father then told us, "You go ahead, and I am going to look for the camera."

We went to the bridge rail and watched in amazement at the swirling river beneath us.

After a while, my father arrived and said, "I couldn't find the camera, it must be packed away."

For some strange reason, I suspected he was not being honest with us. I ran to the car to check on Itsy, and my worst fears were realized. My precious little kitten was gone, and I rushed to Mom and confronted her, "He threw him over the bridge into the river, didn't he?"

She started to cry and could only say, "Yes, I am so sorry."

HELLO, WARSAW

We reached the end of the bridge and were only about eight miles from our destination. Before we left Wytheville, I had tried to get Dad to tell me what to expect in Warsaw. The only thing he would tell me was that I would enjoy living there. I was not convinced and became apprehensive about this major change in my life. As we traversed the final leg of our journey, all I could see on both sides of the road were swamps. Several times I spotted bald eagles perched in tall trees. At first, I was sure there were alligators in the murky waters below. However, I convinced myself that they were old dead tree trunks. At long last we reached the outskirts of town. We all were tired, hot, hungry, and in bad need of a restroom break. We found a restaurant, stopped, and recharged our bodies and our minds. Unfortunately, our dispositions remained in a sad state of irritability.

As we entered the west side of town on Main Street, I did not see anything that got me excited. At first there were only houses on both sides. Suddenly we came to the "business district," which was composed of a drugstore on the left and some other small stores on the right. There was also a large courthouse beside a park, which appeared to be the heart of the town. Just as quickly as we had entered town, we left it heading east. Dad continued to drive out into the countryside. He had previously come to Warsaw to scope out everything and to rent our new home. As we drove away from town, the landscape turned into farms and large fields of crops. Eventually we arrived at our new house, a spacious two-story home. I was impressed until he informed us that we were on the lower level and another family was occupying the upper level. This house was in a rural area with no other homes in sight.

The first several weeks were hectic as we unpacked and became familiar with our surroundings. Since it was summer, Billy and I were out of school and each day was extremely boring. A little girl my age lived upstairs, but as a seven-year-old, I had no interest in girls. I considered them to be nothing more than a nuisance who should be avoided at all cost. As I got older and progressed through the natural growth cycle of life, my attitude toward the opposite sex changed drastically. The hot summer days dragged on as I tried to entertain myself. The only thing that I was able to come up with was to swing on a rope that hung from a tree limb, fly a kite, or to see how many ants I could eliminate by stomping on them. I did not like killing any living thing, but a movie that I saw once showed army ants attacking natives in Africa and eating their eyes out. So I felt that I was justified in eliminating this deadly threat. On Saturdays there was a break in the monotony to go into town for groceries and other various sundry items. While week days were quiet, Saturdays brought crowds of people from the outlying rural areas. Sometimes Mom would leave me on one of the park benches while she shopped and Dad restocked his supply of liquid refreshment. I would sit and watch all the farmers chew tobacco and spit on the ground. Occasionally they would sit next to me and offer to give me a chaw. I would politely reply, "No, thank you, I am trying to cut down!"

So the days passed as summer gave way to fall. As the seasons began changing, the farmers worked their fields. One of them let me ride with him on his tractor, and I have never forgotten his kindness.

Also with fall came another year of school. In Warsaw there was only one school, which housed students ranging from the first grade to the twelfth grade. I entered the second grade determined to get more serious about my school work. Each day we had a one-hour period when we could go outside behind the building for recess. They gave us a variety of options that involved running and exercise. The idea was to burn off some of our energy and restlessness. I chose to play with three other boys who believed that together they could wrestle me to the ground. Since I was much bigger, they always failed. Our contest continued each day for a week until one of the teachers put a stop to it.

Like most of the kids, I had to ride a school bus to and from school every day. My stop was the first one going home after school. I loved to ride the bus, so I made friends with the driver. I convinced him to let me stay on the bus until he reached the end of his route. He would then drop me off on his way back. He was a super guy, and we had many long conversations during those long rides. I remember thinking how different my life would have been if he had been my father. However, even at my age, I realized that sometimes in life you have to make the best of situations that you can't control. When that happens, you take what you have got and you run with it. As I became older and more mature, that theory prepared me to overcome many adversities in my life. I will cover this subject in more detail later in this book. The year flew by, and I made it through the second grade without causing any problems.

One day my dad brought home a small cardboard box, which was only two feet square. It was obvious he was excited and anxious to reveal the contents. He made all three of us sit on the sofa during the unveiling of the mystery item. He carefully cut the box and gently placed the thing on a small table. We quickly determined it was some type of electrical device since it had both a cord and a plug. In the front was a glass window which you could not see through. Next, he plugged it in and pressed the "On" switch. It hummed for a few minutes, and then the window lit up. We all gasped when we saw several little people behind the window looking back at us. At first it was frightening, but we were all right when we determined that we were seeing images and not real people.

Dad explained to us that we were now the proud owners of a wonderful new invention, a television. He explained, "Most people simply call it a TV."

We all clapped and acted excited, but then in unison asked, "WHAT IS THAT THING, AND WHAT DOES IT DO?"

He just kept playing around with the controls and ignoring us. The picture on the screen was fussy and kept flickering. He then looked up and told us, "Just wait until I hook up the rabbit ears."

We all exchanged dumbfounded expressions. He then took out a small box which contained a base that had two rods protruding upward to form a *V*.

He proudly explained to us, "These are the 'rabbit ears,' and they will help us get better reception."

While I was trying to figure all this out, I remembered in school we had studied all kinds of insects. Most of them had antenna sticking out of their heads. It was logical to me that all bugs and insects with antenna also had TVs. I found this new information fascinating, and I wondered what kind of programs they watched. I decided that the next time I had to write and present a research paper, it would be titled, "New Discovery of Insects Watching TV." I was sure the teacher would be impressed that I knew so much on the topic.

WARSAW CONTINUED

The TV turned out to be an exciting electrical invention that would eventually surpass the radio as the primary home entertainment provider. We were fortunate to own one. Programming was limited, and the reception was erratic. There were no cable services back then, and satellites had not been invented. After a year or two, people began attaching large antennae on their roofs. These antennae looked like a conglomeration of coat hangers. Some even came with an electrical cord that was attached to a control box inside the house which enabled the occupant to turn the antennae until a clear picture appeared. The first TV pictures were in black and white only. It was quite some time later that color TV was introduced. If you wanted to add some color to the picture, you could purchase clear plastic-coated sheets which could be stuck on the screen. However, the colors were just stationary patterns which did not match anything appearing on the screen. You might be looking at people with green skins, yellow skies, or red animals. There were usually only three or maybe four channels to select from. Our parents mostly watched news programs or sporting events. Bill and I watched the good stuff, *Howdy Doody* and *Kukla, Fran and Ollie*. *Howdy Doody* was a kids show staring Howdy Doody who was a string puppet along with several other puppets. Along with the puppets were some real characters, Buffalo Bob, Clarabell the Clown, and an Indian named Princess Summer Fall Winter Spring. *Kukla, Fran and Ollie* featured hand puppets and a young lady. Both shows in today's standards would be far down on the list of quality entertainment. Kids in our present culture with all the technology and movies like *Star Wars* and various superheroes would think shows like *Howdy Doody* and *Kukla, Fran and Ollie* were totally silly and they would be correct. However, it was all we had at the time, and we didn't know any better. We were more fortunate than most kids we knew whose parents did not own a TV.

WARSAW, THE FINAL MONTHS

In the summer after I had finished the second grade we moved again. This time we moved into town to a house on Main Street that my dad had rented. It was a few miles from "downtown," but was within walking distance of the stores and shops. What was more important to Billy and me was that we were finally living in a neighborhood with other kids. It was our opportunity to meet and make friends with others we could enjoy playing with. It seemed like things were really looking up. It did not take long for the "local kids" to find out there were two new boys living on Main Street. We quickly became full-fledged members of the neighborhood gang. Once we joined the others, the group totaled ten boys. Their names were Bert, Nick, Kinky, George, Sam, Bob, and two brothers, Tommy and Johnny. Most of the others were a little older than me, but that did not make any difference since Billy was three years my senior. Billy and I both talked about how great it was to be with other boys our age. As is the case with any "organization," "the gang" had a mixture of characters with varied personalities. Some of them were leaders, and some were followers. Since Billy was more mature than the others, I would classify him as one of the leaders. The self-appointed leader was Bert. He was one of those individuals who thought he knew everything and claimed he had done everything. The rest of us gave him the name Braggart Bert. The rest of the boys were fun to be with, but they would be candidates for a "participation trophy." Tommy and Johnny became our best friends, and we spent most of our time with them.

Since Warsaw was such a small town, there was not much going on for kids like us to do. The highlight of the week for us was going to the movies at a theater located on a side street downtown. Mom let me go as long as I stayed with Billy and the others. Most of the times we went with the brothers, Tommy and Johnny. Since they were older than me, she trusted them to take care of me. It was a long walk from our house to get to the theater, but we were energetic, and we made each trip an adventure. When I went to the theater in Wytheville, it was to see my cowboy heroes in westerns. We were older now, and our favorites were horror movies and science-fiction thrillers. Most of the movies back then would now be graded as low-grade unrealistic B pictures according to the high-tech standards of today. However, they were believable and extremely frightening to us. It was easy to imagine what we saw on the big screen in movies such as *It Came from Outer Space*, *The Day the Earth Stood Still*, and *Invasion of the Body Snatchers* was real. We also enjoyed pushing our "fear button" by sitting through horror films such as *Dracula*, and *The House on Haunted Hill*. One of my favorite monster movies was *The Creature from the Black Lagoon*. As far as our movie preference was concerned, the scarier the better. It was always dark when we got out of the theater, and during the long walk home our thoughts and conversations were still about what we had just seen. The others always carried flashlights, and I felt safe staying close to them. Our route home took us around the perimeter of a church and a large adjoining cemetery. Unknown to me, the others one night had planned to play a cruel trick on me. They informed me that they were going to take a shortcut through the graveyard. I was scared, but I had no choice if I wanted to get home. We had traveled halfway through the cemetery when they suddenly turned off their flashlights, scattered in different direction, and left me alone in the dark. They then hid behind tombstones and monuments and started making all kinds of scary sounds. I pleaded for them to come back, and after getting a good laugh at my expense, they rejoined me, and we completed our return home. Billy made sure I would not tell Mom what happened by threatening to convince her to never let me go to the movies again until I was older. About two weeks later, when we left the theater, they stated that they wanted to take the same cemetery shortcut. They silenced my objections by promising to not leave me this time. Too late, my fears were realized, and I found myself alone next to a headstone. Instead of panicking, this time I sat down and leaned against a headstone of some guy named Niamiah Hornsby. Eventually my companions got tired of making silly sounds and reappeared. I let them know how mean they were, and then I gave them a challenge to never do this again or they would regret it. I was smart enough to know they would try something, and I was already planning my revenge. It did not take long, and we were off to the movies again. They did not try anything walking to the theater nor during the movie. Just as I had hoped, it looked like the graveyard was going to be the battleground. I could not believe they were going to try to pull the same old trick a third time. They lived up to my low expectations, and as soon as their flashlights went off, I sprang into action. From my pants pocket, I snapped on a small flashlight, turned around, and headed out the way we had just come in. On the way in, I had made a mental note of our route using tombstones as landmarks. With my first steps back on the streets, I broke into a sprint for home. My plan was to arrive at home before they did since, for a while, they would be searching for me in the cemetery. Mom would be furious when I got home without them. Even if they beat me home, how would they explain why I was not with them or where I was? As it turned out, the plan worked to perfection. Mom wanted to know where Billy and our friends were. I was honest and told her I did not know since they had run away from me. It was quite some time before Billy got home. Mom had told me to go into the bedroom and close the door. She let him think that I had never come home before she lit into him. The yelling went on for a while before she rendered her punishment. He was grounded for a month and could not leave the house except to attend church (which meant no movies). In the meantime, she would take me and any friends that I wanted to invite to the movies and pick us up. It seemed like a fair decision to me.

More Warsaw Adventures

There were more adventures with our friends that I remember vividly.

One year several of the boys received air rifles, also known as BB guns, and we had a good time shooting at tin cans. If you are not familiar with these rifles, they fire a BB, which is a tiny round "bullet." The shooter would load these BBs in the gun and then would cock it, creating a chamber of compressed air. When the trigger was pulled, the compressed air would propel the BB. The most popular BB gun was the Daisy replica of the Winchester rifle, which was commonly referred to as the "gun which won the West." These rifles were quite accurate and could be lethal if not used with caution. Billy got one for Christmas, and one day he shot a robin and killed it. He immediately realized what he had done and buried it. He was distraught over this for a long time and never shot another bird or any living thing. However, Bert considered himself to be a big game hunter and was constantly shooting at the birds. The rest of us let him know that we did not approve of this and told him that someday the birds would get their revenge.

One day after school, we were all walking home, and our prophecy came true. Bert had bought a large lollipop and was busy licking it. We heard a bird which was sitting on a limb in a nearby tree start chirping and screeching. Suddenly it took off and started a nosedive toward Bert. It pulled out of its dive right above Bert, and it was "bombs away." It was a direct hit on the sucker. Bert, in a rage, threw the lollipop away and had some choice words for the dive-bombing bird. We were rolling on the ground laughing so hard our sides hurt.

When I looked up, I saw the bird perched in another tree. It was making a weird noise, which was even louder than us. To this day I believe it was laughing right along with us.

Another time during the summer, four of us were playing together when Bert told us he knew where there was a large fishpond back in the woods. He wanted to go there and try to shoot some frogs. The rest of us thought it would be a fun thing to do, and we followed him into the woods. Bert and Kinky had their air rifles with them. When we finally reached the pond, we discovered that it was much larger than Bert had described. We found an old rowboat sitting on the shore that did not look like it could float. However, it had two oars in it, so we decided it would be safe to set sail. We had rowed out halfway across the lake when Bert yelled for us to look on some flat rocks on the other shore. What he had seen was a large snake sunning itself. Bert recognized it to be a cottonmouth water moccasin, and Kinky confirmed this, adding they were very aggressive and poisonous. With this thought in mind, the two of them opened up on the serpent with their rifles. We watched as BB after BB hit the snake but did not puncture its thick skin. Suddenly it darted off the rocks, hit the water, and headed for our boat. It glided across the surface at a great speed. We sat there helplessly awaiting our fate as the snake came closer and closer. I thought about jumping overboard, but I did not know how to swim. It seemed as if I would die either from a snake bite or by drowning. As I watched the viper approach, it reminded me of how sailors during the war felt while watching a German torpedo headed toward their ship. Suddenly the snake was at the side of the boat as we all sat there frozen in fear. It effortlessly crawled up the side and into the boat. We were still as stone statues as it slithered between our feet. Before we could catch our breath, it slid up and over the other side back into the water. We gave out a collective sigh as we watched it swim to the shore and disappear into the underbrush. It seemed like a long time before we rowed back to shore and beached the boat in the grass. As we hiked back home, I made myself two promises. First of all, I was never going to return to that pond. The second promise I made was more important. I vowed to never again challenge Mother Nature or the creatures with whom we share our planet earth.

One hot day I was riding my bike, and a small insect flew in my ear. I could not get it out, and it proceeded to bore its way deeper into my ear canal. I could feel it moving around, and it was driving me crazy. It must have been tiny, but it felt like it was the size of a grasshopper. My imagination ran rampant as I visualized it entering my brain and crawling all the way across my skull and out my other ear. Fortunately, I sought some adult help before that occurred. Mom did not have a clue as what to do, so she found a neighbor who lived next door. He got an eyedropper and sprayed some kind of warm oil in the ear. Not only did the insect not retreat, it climbed even deeper. By this time some other people showed up, and one of them came up with a "bright idea" (no pun intended). He explained that insects were attracted to light and warmth. For example, the old saying "like a moth to a flame." He got a small pen flashlight, turned it on, and placed it in the ear canal as far as he could. At first nothing happened, but then I began to feel some movement. The insect was definitely on the move, but the question was, in what direction? Slowly it eventually appeared and flew away once the light was removed. Even to this day, I often think about this incident. Based on some decisions that I made later in life, I wonder if that poor little insect did, indeed, damage part of my brain.

In the summer following my completion of the fourth grade, Dad learned that he was being transferred once again. This time it was to Salem, a small city located in the Roanoke Valley in southwestern Virginia. My experiences in Warsaw were about to end, and a new era awaited me in Salem.

However, I have one last story to tell before I say goodbye to Warsaw. Behind our home across some fields was an old abandoned house that we could see. Years of neglect had taken its toll on what must have originally been a beautiful estate. Now everything had deteriorated to the point of extinction. The front yard was surrounded by an old, rusty fence that had sections missing and a gate which hung from one hinge. Vines and greenery hung in layers covering up most of the siding and roof. Windows were broken, and shutters were open, allowing drapes inside to be visible. I am sure this description brings to mind a certain type of house. If you guessed a "haunted house," you are exactly right. The movie makers could not have made a more accurate one.

At nights Billy and I would join our friends and intently watch the old house across the fields. We were alert for any movement, any sign of life or any sign of the dead. Everyone had a different tale about seeing eerie and spooky things. One kid swore he had once seen lit candles through the windows. Another one said he had also seen the candles, but they were being carried from room to room. Several of them stated that they had heard strange noises and screams. Still another tried to convince us that he had seen people or ghosts wearing white shrouds peering back at him out of the windows. All of us agreed that sometimes the shutters were open and other times they were closed. No one was brave enough to go near the place.

One night Bert and two other boys bragged that they were not only going over there, they were going inside. We challenged them to prove it, but only if we could witness it. They agreed, and the date and time were set. We decided to all meet at the edge of the fields at 9:00 PM on Wednesday of the following week. This was going to be one of the biggest events of our summer, and we could hardly wait for the upcoming "fright night." The big night came, and we were all there waiting for our three heroes to join us.

If this book was fiction, this story would be more interesting. I would be telling you that our three ghost chasers arrived on time and proceeded across the fields to the haunted house. Next, I would describe how we watched them walk up the creaky old steps and disappear into the dilapidated structure. Then I would reveal what they found inside and what happened to each of them. Maybe you would learn that they never returned and their fate is still a mystery.

However, this book is a true and honest story of my life. So what did happen to these three "brave" souls? We waited for them to show up for an hour and finally accepted the fact that they weren't coming. In the next few days we confronted all three. One said he got sick, one said his parents made him go to church, and the remaining one simply said he "chickened out."

INTERMISSION

The Warsaw chapter of my life had now ended, and now it was off to the next adventure. Dad had once again been transferred by the Highway Department. Our new home will be in Salem, Virginia, which was back to the southwestern part of the state. However, it would not be as far west as Wytheville. I would soon find out that Salem was located in the Roanoke Valley along with the City of Roanoke and another small town, Vinton. The Valley was surrounded by several outlying counties. They are Roanoke County, Montgomery County, Botetourt County, Bedford County, and Franklin County. Little did I know at the time that I would spend most of the next fifty years of my life living in the Roanoke Valley.

Most people in their lives are effected by serious events and situations which can be either wonderful or tragic. Usually these are referred to as "game-changing" or "life-changing." As you are about to learn, in my life I have experienced many of these changes.

In the stories of my life as a youngster, I presented what I would describe as *Tom Sawyer & Huckleberry Finn* type tales. We have now arrived at the important history of my life. It begins with our arrival in Salem, which I have always considered to be a "life-changing" experience.

HELLO, SALEM

Our move to Salem was uneventful. We had grown familiar with the routine of moving from one city to another and to different houses once we got settled. The step-by-step process was to pack up our belongings, hire some men to haul our furniture, drive to the destination, unpack everything, and begin getting familiar with our new surroundings. However, this time it all seemed different to me. Maybe it was because I was a little more mature, or perhaps, I sensed that something drastic was going to occur in my life.

Our new rental residence was located in a section on the outskirts of Salem named Fort Lewis. There were other homes in the neighborhood, but the entire time we lived there, I only made friends with one boy. Below our house and across a highway was the site of Andrew Lewis's home. You notice I said *site*, not home. His home had been destroyed years ago, but the grounds were being maintained as a memorial to him. Most people are not familiar with Andrew Lewis. He was a famous pioneer, soldier, and statesman during the colonial era in American history. He was an officer in the militia during the French and Indian War and also served as a brigadier general under George Washington in the American Revolution. He died in 1781 and is buried in a Salem cemetery. The city had apparently adopted him as their "favorite son." There is a highway named after him, and the high school that I would later attend was Andrew Lewis High School.

It did not take long to settle in to our normal routine at home. Dad's addiction to booze went from bad to worse. Our parents were constantly fighting with each other. It was always about either his drinking or financial problems. A short time after we arrived in Salem, it was time for school to start. I attended the fifth grade at Fort Lewis Elementary, and Billy started in the eighth grade at Andrew Lewis High School. The school year for me passed quickly without anything significant happening. However, before the summer could get started, it was time to pack up again. This time we were moving to another house located in the "South Salem" area. I was beginning to see a pattern in my life. In three years, I had moved three times and attended three different schools. What I didn't know at the time was that it would soon be four moves and four different schools.

SOUTH SALEM

I was glad when we made the move from Fort Lewis to South Salem. It was closer in town and there were a lot of other kids my age that lived near us. Our house was on a comer of an intersection and was only a few blocks from the school. There was a large open area next to the building which had a baseball field. There were always a group of kids to play a game of pick up baseball or touch football.

One day I was alone in my front yard, playing with a rubber ball. I noticed a kid walking down the street toward me.

When he got closer, he walked over and said, "Hello, I am Charlie. Can I play with your ball?"

I answered, "Sure, I am Jimmy, and I just moved here."

As fate would have it, he became my best friend. Even though we now live in different parts of Virginia, we stay in touch and we talk on the phone a couple of times a week. Charlie was an outstanding athlete who played sandlot football and baseball. I wanted to play football, but they had a rule that you could not weigh over a certain amount. They said it was a regulation to keep the smaller players from getting hurt. In all honesty, I was not only overweight; I was just plain fat. It was disappointing, but I did go to watch Charlie play. However, I did play sandlot baseball for two years. My team was the South Salem Lions, and I played three different positions, first base, pitcher, and catcher.

A couple of summers and the fifth grade passed without much significant happening. Dad and Mom continued to fight, and Dad spent each night with his two friends, Jim Beam and Jack Daniels. Of course, we moved again several times. Although I did not understand what it meant at the time, Billy told me that we were evicted due to Dad's addiction.

SALEM ONWARD
AND UPWARD

For the seventh grade I attended Broad Street Elementary. It was my last school prior to entering high school. I don't recall that it was any different from my previous six years. After the school year ended, we made yet another move.

This time Dad had rented a home located on a street named Upland Drive. It was a few miles East of Salem in a nice neighborhood. However, there were no children living on our street. It turned out to be a rather boring and uneventful summer. I was really excited to start school again. This year I would be in the eighth grade and would be a student at Andrew Lewis High School. Although eighth graders were still considered to be a bunch of little kids by the upperclass students, it was a big deal for us. Instead of having one teacher and one class room all day, you had a homeroom in the morning with a teacher. She would record our attendance, which only took about a half an hour. The bell would then sound for us to go to our first class in another part of the building. Each class was approximately an hour long, and most students were taking four classes a day. In addition to that, we were required to take a physical education class, also known as gym class. Our day at school also included a lunch hour and a study hall. For those of us who the faculty determined needed some discipline training, there was the "tardy hall." If you had broken the rules or had misbehaved, you were sentenced to stay after school for a certain length of time based on the severity of your offense. For offenses even more serious, you could be suspended from school for three days. One would think that was not a punishment since you would have a break from school. However, during the time you missed class, you would have to make up any homework assignments that had been assigned during your absence. I will have to admit that I was not a perfect student when it came to my work ethic and my behavior. My habits when it came to classroom accomplishments were a holdover from my elementary school days. I had the intelligence, but lacked the motivation to excel. I was satisfied to just get by with passing grades. This presented a problem for me. Billy was three years ahead of me in school, and he also had many of the same teachers that I now had. As I have previously stated, he was "Mr. Perfect" in everything he did. He was an honor student with straight As on all his report cards. I came along and was not able to match his legacy. All I heard from the teachers was, "Jimmy, I was disappointed in your paper [or test]. Billy always did much better."

As far as getting in trouble with the teachers and the administrators, I would say I graded out to a C+. While I got into a little hot water during my years in high school, I was never dishonest or did anything to hurt anyone else. In my first year at Andrew Lewis, my homeroom teacher was Mary Jane Maxwell. I also had her for a science class later in the day. She was young, attractive, single, and I had a silly crush on her. One morning I noticed that she had a cute pair of earrings on. That afternoon when I went to her class; I noticed that she was wearing a different pair.

Toward the end of class, she said, "Well, our time is all most up. Does anyone have a question about what we covered today?" When my hand shot up, she nodded and said, "Yes, Jimmy, what is it?"

I replied, "I was wondering why you changed the earrings you had on this morning." She hesitated for a second while she digested my insolence. Then she flew into a rage, glared at me, and yelled, "Everyone out immediately when the bell rings! Jimmy, you stay in your seat."

After several agonizing minutes, the bell rang, and the room quickly cleared. It appeared she had calmed down at least a little. She slowly walked back to my desk, leaned over, and got up in my face. I was about to swoon when I smelled her perfume. However, instead I braced for the oncoming lecture I was about to receive.

Her first sentence got right to the point when she said, "You do not ever talk to a teacher or any lady like that. It is none of your business what I wear or when I wear it. You are just a young kid, and you have a lot to learn about women. DO YOU UNDERSTAND WHAT I AM TELLING YOU?"

I calmly answered, "Yes, you have made it very clear."

She then turned to walk away while telling me, "You may leave now."

I arose from my seat and headed for the door. When I got halfway through the door, I turned and said, "By the way, the earrings you had on this morning looked a lot better."

I was out the door and down the hall before she had time to get up from her desk. The next day, she didn't look my way during homeroom. I felt guilty and decided to try to make amends with her. At lunch, they had a big bowl of assorted fruit on the food line. I picked out the biggest and reddest apple I could find. When the bell rang at the end of the last class of the day, I sprinted to her room to catch her before she left. I found her still at her desk grading some test papers. She looked up with a puzzled look on her face when I said, "I want to apologize for what I said to you the other day. It would have been bad enough in private, but to embarrass you in front of the class was terrible. I hope you will forgive me. I brought you a nice apple to show you I am sincere."

She looked at me with a disgusted look, but suddenly a big grin came across her face. She exclaimed, "I was mad at school, but when I went home, it seemed funny when I thought about it. It is very kind of you to bring me an apple and to let me know how you feel. You are forgiven, and let's be friends the rest of the year. Goodbye, I will see you tomorrow."

I turned and headed for the door. I had reached about halfway when I heard her say in a loud voice, "Oh, by the way, you still have a lot to learn about girls and women."

We got along just fine the rest of the year. However, I got into a bit of trouble in the eighth grade with the principal, Dewitt Miller. I took a "fake" camera to school one day. It looked like a real camera but was actually a water gun. It was a lot of fun to ask someone if you could take their picture. When they posed, you clicked the camera, and they wound up with a face full of water. One of the teachers found out and took the camera away from me. Several days went by, and no one mentioned it, so I figured I was off the hook. The next day after that, a student knocked on the door to a class I was in and handed a folded-up note to the teacher. She opened it, read it, and looked at me. Then she said, "Jimmy, you need to go to Mr. Miller's office immediately."

When I arrived his office door was closed and his secretary told me, "Have a seat, Mr. Miller will be with you shortly."

It was about twenty minutes before he opened the door. He had laid out on the top of his desk a multitude of items. There was a slingshot, a switchblade knife, a small transistor radio, and a medicine bottle among other items.

He asked, "Which one of these is yours?"

"The little camera, it shoots water when you click it."

He picked it up and began turning it over, examining it. 'How does it work?"

"Give it to me, and I will show you."

"No, we are not going to play that game. I have decided that I am not going to punish you, but I am going to keep the camera."

I left his office, wondering if his wife was going to get her picture taken when he got home.

ALHS FRESHMAN YEAR

I got through the eighth grade without any other problems. My grades improved each report card period, but some were still mostly Cs. It all depended on whether or not I liked the subject and also who the teacher was. My best subjects were history, English, and some sciences. I struggled with all math classes.

The second semester ended, and it was time for a break. I spent most of the summer playing in pickup baseball games with my friends. It was nice to have a vacation from my studies, but at the same time, I was looking forward to next year when I would be a high school student. It would be in the same building, and I would have my own locker. It would also give me an opportunity to be involved with clubs, sports, and other school activities.

However, my family could not get through the summer without a "game-changing" event. As usual, it involved my dad. We didn't think his drinking addiction could get any worse, but we were wrong. It always amazed me that he could consume a fifth of bourbon each night and then get up and go in to work each morning. We had one car we owned, and the Highway Department furnished him with a company vehicle. As far as I knew, he had never driven the company car except to work. Sometimes he drove our personal car while drinking, but rarely.

One night around midnight, he got in his company car and drove away in a drunken condition. He didn't get far when he went off the road and over an embankment. He didn't get hurt, but the car was totaled. When his superior at the Highway Department found out, he fired Dad. Dad wasted no time in both applying for another job and resuming his drinking. After interviewing with other companies, he was hired by a local paving company.

We made it through the summer without anything else drastic happening. However, the booze continued to flow each night. It seemed like he got soused quicker, which meant he also got meaner. There were times we had to hide in some woods behind the house to avoid his mental and physical abuse. One night the three of us ran out of the house to get away in the car. As we were pulling out of the driveway, he ran out of the house, leaped on the front of the car, raised the hood, and jerked the carburetor wires loose. For us the rest of the night was spent trying to avoid him and hoping he would soon pass out. It felt like waiting in the woods for a bear to attack. For some reason he left us alone, and he left early for work before we got up.

As always, the summer break flew by, and it was time to report for the first day of school. A lot of the students were the same ones I knew from the eighth grade, but a few were new to the school. I mingled with everyone, but I found that I was not popular. I had a good idea as to why this was the case. At this time, I was grossly overweight and extremely self-conscious. As a result, I was shy and not fun to be with. The guys considered me to be "not cool," and I had little to offer the girls. Instead of trying to do anything about it, I accepted my fate, but I tried to be kind and friendly to everyone. My philosophy was to remain genuine instead of trying to be something I was not. So my freshman year, I was a happy-go-lucky kind of guy. Despite my shortcomings, I turned out to be a rather likeable kid, or so it seemed to me. Salem was a big sports city, and the support of Andrew Lewis by the parents and the citizens was phenomenal. I tried to attend as many football and basketball games that I could. With all that was going on, it turned out to be a lot of fun. Then came another summer, followed by my sophomore year. However, before the new school year, my family experienced a "life changer."

SEPTEMBER 1957 8:14 PM

The year was 1957, I was fifteen years old and beginning my sophomore year of high school. My mom and my brother, Billy, were at the high school attending "back-to-school night." This was something that was done annually at the beginning of the school year. It gave the parents a chance to meet their children's teachers and to ask any questions they might have. I had not gone with them in order to concentrate on some overdue homework assignments. I decided to take a break and went to the front living room. There was a terrible storm brewing outside, and I sat down to watch it playing havoc with the trees. We had one tall tree in the front yard, which was being whipped back and forth by the relentless gale. My dad was somewhere else in the house, and I was glad to be alone. He had been moody at supper and had nothing to say to any of us. Since then the night had taken on an eerie ominous atmosphere. It caused me to be overcome by a deep sense of foreboding. Little did I know that my life was about to be changed forever.

Suddenly I heard footsteps behind me as Dad walked toward the porch door. He never looked my way or uttered a word as he passed. Once he got outside, he seemed to be in no hurry as he walked slowly through the raging storm to his car. He got in, started the car, and just sat there; it appeared to me that he was in some kind of daze brought on by indecision. In an instant I heard what sounded like a gunshot. I watched in horror as his head snapped back. Seconds later, I realized that we both had reacted to loud thunder and lightning, which split the big tree in half. As the tree broke, he had jerked his hand up, and it appeared that he had waved at me. However, in the same motion, he slammed the car into reverse and raced away. I watched in disbelief as the car's red taillights faded away in the night.

We never saw or heard from him again. He was out of our lives forever. Mom could not cope with the tragedy, and six months later she had a nervous breakdown and had to be committed to a mental institution. Billy and I were now alone and were basically orphans. It was up to the two of us to overcome the challenge of survival.

LIFE AFTER DAD

After my dad left on that stormy night, it took us several days to determine he was not coming back. We had to accept the fact that the three of us were experiencing a "life-changing" event. At the time, I had mixed emotions. I felt a great relief that none of us would have to suffer the "hell" he had created for us. At the same time, I also realized that we had a tough time ahead of us.

As I think back on the entire scenario, I now think Mom knew this was going to happen. She and Dad had a heated argument the night before. When she and Billy got home, she did not act surprised at all. After that she did hold out hope that he might return. It was confirmed that he was gone for good when she found that he had taken some of his clothes and personal items. The clincher came when she tried to take some money out of the bank account and was told that he had withdrawn all but one dollar.

We sat down and tried to formulate a plan for our future. It was my sophomore year in school, and I was only fifteen, so I could not help much financially. Mom was substituting for another teacher who was on a medical leave of absence until the spring. Billy was a senior and would graduate in June. He offered to take a part-time job and was able to get on at Kroger. He had planned to go to college at Virginia Tech after graduation. My immediate future was to finish high school and go to college if we could afford it. It seemed like a feasible plan on paper, but sometimes the best of plans don't materialize.

Our Mom could not handle the strain of teaching and the destruction of her marriage. She suffered mentally and eventually was diagnosed as having a nervous breakdown. In March she was committed to a mental institution in Staunton, Virginia. Billy and I were now on our own, which called for a new plan. There was some money in the bank we could use, but we had to somehow generate more income than his part-time job produced. We had about two and half months until he graduated. If we could get through until June, he could start working full-time instead of going to college. At that point I would have two years left before I graduated and started to work full-time. Hopefully, this would enable him to then attend college full-time or part-time. We decided to move to a smaller house and were able to find one only two blocks from the high school. The rent was less, and we found out that our parents were required to pay a security deposit of two months. That was returned to us when we moved, so that took care of two months for the new house. Once the school year ended, I did get a part-time job for the summer bagging groceries at Kroger.

The summer was not the usual break for us. We both were trying to earn as much money as we could. Billy was disappointed that he would not be able to go away to college. I promised him that after I graduated, I would get a decent job and he could enroll at Virginia Tech. Of course, we were concerned about Mom, and we made several trips to Staunton to visit her. Neither one of us ever talked about Dad, and I had quickly put him out of my mind. As far as our friends were concerned, they had no idea we were basically "orphans." Because we had no parents, we also had no rules, no restrictions, no supervision, and no guidance. As I now think back, we were free to do anything we wanted to do. We could have lived a wild life and wound up in a lot trouble. Instead we lived a clean, healthy lifestyle. Neither of us drank, smoked, or used drugs. When your life suddenly changes and you are faced with what seems to be an insurmountable adversity, you transform from a "boy" to a "man" in a hurry. I know this event made me stronger and prepared me for future trials and tribulations in my life.

FOOTBALL 101

In the summer prior to my junior year in high school, my best friend, Charlie, encouraged me to go out for the football team. He was an outstanding athlete who excelled in all sports. I gave it a lot of consideration and decided to give it a try. It turned out to be not only the right decision but a "life changer" as well. Up to that point, my life at school had been very difficult. I was grossly overweight, self-conscious, and embarrassed at how I looked. As far as I could tell, most of the students didn't know that I existed. Practice started in early August, almost a month before the first day of school. Practice was grueling in the high ninety-degree heat. The coaches had us getting in three practices a day. It was especially challenging for me since I weighed 317 pounds and was out of shape. Yes, I said 300, not two hundred. I worked hard and was determined to stick with it. When the team was allowed to take a break, I was on the sideline doing sit-ups. As the days passed, I began to lose the fat and replace it with muscle. Back in those days if you had linemen weighing two hundred pounds, you were fortunate. The game has really changed since then. A lot of linemen now are over three hundred pounds, and the running backs are two hundred pounds. I often wondered how the other team felt when they saw me trot out on the field. Actually, I was not very good, but I was big so I got to play a lot.

Someone a long time ago asked me, "If you were an animal, what would you want to be?" I didn't hesitate when I answered, "A cheetah!" The reason I wanted to be a cheetah (and still do) is because they are one of the swiftest animals in the world. A grown cheetah reaches speeds of up to seventy-six miles per hour. They also have great acceleration and can hit sixty miles an hour in only three seconds. I have a large framed photograph of a cheetah on my wall at home. You may be wondering what this has to do with football. In addition to being "big," I was also slow.

Our head coach Hal Johnston once told me, "Cecil, you run fast, but you run in one spot too long."

He also staged a fifty-yard race at one of our practices between his ten-year-old son Hal Jr. and me. It wasn't even close. I took off with a blast from the start, and the gap between us increased with every stride. I could hear my teammates cheering me on, and I felt like this was going to be my day of glory. As I neared the finish line, they were all screaming, including Little Hal, who was waiting for me to arrive.

I quickly forgot the embarrassing defeat and concentrated on learning the fine art of playing football. Basically you can defeat your opponent if you are stronger, faster, and smarter. After meeting some of my teammates, I was having doubts if they were qualifying for the third requirement. What I couldn't figure out was whether or not they were born that way or was it the result of playing football. For all you guys that were my teammates, I apologize for that comment. Every one of you were and are still great friends. My life is better for knowing you.

All too soon it was time to begin the new school year, and I faced it with newfound confidence. Now I had fifty new friends, my teammates. We were the Wolverines and proud of it. Midway through the first week, there was a big assembly in the auditorium, and each member of the team was introduced to the faculty and the student body. Just that quickly I went from being a "nobody" to being a "hero." With each week of practice and game experience, I got better. We played our games on Friday nights. Each Monday when I would arrive at school, I would have people all day long congratulating me and telling me what a great game I had played. I really had not reached the level that I felt like I was great, but I was not seeking greatness. I enjoyed playing football, even though we did not have a super year. We won four games, lost four games, and tied two games. However, when we played the Jefferson High School Magicians, a Roanoke team, we ended a jinx that had endured since 1946. They were the "big dogs" among Virginia high schools. We were a decisive underdog, yet we managed to tie them 13–13. It was not a win, but it was a moral victory for the City of Salem fans. The season ended all too soon, and the games were just a memory in the record books. The practices were over, there were no more games to play, and it was time to turn in our equipment. Each year a banquet was given in our honor, monogram letters were given to those who had earned them, and special awards were presented. I was not expecting anything but was awarded a trophy for being "the Most Deserving Substitute" by Don Oakes, a professional football player for both the Philadelphia Eagles and the Boston Patriots. It was a total surprise and a wonderful way to end my first year of organized football.

The rest of my junior school year awaited me. It was time to hit the books, begin practice of another sport, and get to know the ladies.

This was a newspaper photo taken of me on the first day of football practice in 1957.

SITTIN' THIS ONE OUT—"Don't wait for me, fellas," groans the well padded lad who's holding his head. He found no moderation yesterday in the first day of football drills—too much running and too much of Mother Nature's heat treatment.

THE REST OF MY JUNIOR YEAR

Each football player was required to play basketball, or another sport during the year, if he was planning on returning for the next season. The purpose was to keep you in shape for the entire year. However, there were not many other sports available. Andrew Lewis, like most other high schools, had in addition to football only track and basketball. Back then there were no sports for girls. They could, however, participate in cheerleading, the marching band, or chasing guys.

My basketball skills were almost nonexistent, so that left track and field. There were several versions of track based on the time of year and the types of events. For example, cross-country track held meets in the fall and the competitors were all long-distance runners. The "track" was actually more of a trail which ran up and down hills through fields and woods. It consisted of one race to determine the finishing times of the winners. The other two types of track meets were "indoor track" and "outdoor track." The names of each one explain the difference in the two. "Indoor track" meets were held inside huge buildings that were spacious enough to house a quarter-mile track, a pole vault, and broad jump runway, a shot put circle, and landing area. These meets were normally scheduled during the midwinter months. The "outdoor" meets were held during the spring and early summer months. Many of the events held in the indoor facility were the same. With no size constraints, many more events were available, such as longer races. Also in addition to the shot put were the discus-, hammer-, and javelin-throwing competitions.

We were all examined, tested, and put through trials to determine what would give us the best chance to help the team win meets.

They didn't need to test me for my running or jumping skills. However, they made me run different events starting with a hundred-yard dash and continuing through the two-hundred-yard race and the four forty. Just for fun they made me run a mile. To no one's surprise, they decided that the shot put and the discus were my best events. This year's track team included many of the guys who played football. Several of them were big linemen who had a couple of years' experience. What this meant to me was that I would practice every day and be entered in a few meets every once in a while. It also meant that I was on the team to basically stay in shape and continue to lose weight. However, I put forth a maximum effort and enjoyed being on the team.

We did not have a track at Andrew Lewis, so we used one belonging to Roanoke College, a small college located about a mile away in Salem. Part of our track practice was to jog all the way to the college after we dressed at the high school. One day I finished practice, returned to school, showered, dressed, and started to walk home. A teammate of mine, Dewitt, was walking with me. Across from the main school building, there was another smaller building where classes were also held. It was known as the annex. As we walked by the front, we noticed a Volkswagen Beetle parked on the curb. I slowed down and took a long look at it.

The conversation went like this:

"Hey, Jimmy, are you thinking the same thing I am thinking?

"I believe I am, let's do it."

We set our textbooks down and stepped off the curb.

"Front or back?" I asked.

"The engine is in the back, so that is going to be the heaviest."

We each got on a side at the front, lifted it up a little, and swung it up on the sidewalk. The back was a different story. We had to lift it up and set it down continuously a little at a time until we had the car entirely on the walk. We had barely accomplished our goal and were admiring our handiwork when a cop came screeching up in his cruiser.

He leaped out and hollered, "What do you kids think you are doing?"

I responded, "We just wanted to see if we could pick this car up and set it on the sidewalk, Officer. If you would like, we can put it back."

"No! You don't touch it again!" he yelled.

All of a sudden, the annex door opened, and out came one of our teachers, Mr. Roberts (not a real name).

"What have these boys done?" he asked.

When the officer told him what we had done, he replied, "We need to take them over to see the principal."

So we were marched over to the principal's office, only to find that he had left for the day. The assistant principal, Mr. Jenkins (not a real name), greeted us instead and patiently listened to the entire story.

He said, "I am not sure what we need to do with these boys."

The officer spoke up, "I can take them in and have them be charged, and they will have to appear in juvenile court."

"I don't think that will be necessary. We can take care of it here," Mr. Jenkins replied.

As it turned out, Dewitt and I were suspended for three days. However, Dewitt's father was the vice mayor of Salem, and he was back in school the next day while I sat at home.

The track season came to an end, followed by the final days of my junior year. Next up would be the summer break and then my senior year of school. My last year at Andrew Lewis was promising to be a busy one. First of all, there was another season of football. Then I would have to make a decision about going out for track. Toward the end of the second semester, a decision would have to be made pertaining to whether or not I would try to go to college or go to work.

Senior Year 1959–1960

Football practice started in early August as usual. The coaches loved to have us out there during the hottest days of the year. The players assembled, and we all had a brief time to greet each other and catch up on what we had done during the summer. It was obvious we were missing a lot of our best players who had graduated and were now playing for colleges. It was going to be tough to fill their positions.

The coaches had a new practice program lined up for us. The first week consisted mostly of conditioning drills and running a few plays. They also informed us that our second week of practice would be spent at a small college in Lynchburg, Virginia. Lynchburg was about sixty miles away and would take us an hour and a half to get there. We would be bused to the campus and would be housed in the dormitories. The students who were enrolled there would not be on campus until September. We would be fed all our meals by the regular cafeteria staff. Our team would utilize all their practice facilities, and we would be restricted from leaving the campus.

Any of our players who were expecting a "vacation" were in for a rude awakening. Each day there we had three long practices beginning early in the morning. In fact, they were so early we had to wait in the locker rooms in our uniforms for the sun to come up. In between these practices, we squeezed in three meals, had "chalk talks," and took care of injuries. "Chalk talks" were classroom sessions spent studying plays, discussing strategies, and watching game films. In addition, the coaches would use this time to address any concerns they might have.

After this week was up, we rode back to Salem to prepare for the start of school and our first home game. It was great to finally hit an opponent instead of your own teammates. However, we did not have a wonderful season and finished with four wins and six losses. I only played on defense (when the other team has the ball), and I was either a defensive tackle or a noseguard. The tackle lines up at the "line of scrimmage" across from the other team's tackle. If our defense was in a different formation, the noseguard would line up on the other team's center. The center on a team was usually one of the best players since he had to hike the ball to a back, usually the quarterback, and then block a defensive player. Although we did not have a winning season, I still remember the exhilaration of competing and the satisfaction of accomplishment. Those were special times spent with my teammates that I will always cherish.

Since I was graduating and would no longer be in school the next season, it was unnecessary to spend the second semester on the track team. I thought about giving it another try, but decided that I had to be realistic and accept the fact that I was not good enough to make the team. However, I figured out another way to be a part of the team. I applied to be an equipment manager and was selected. As an equipment manager, you were responsible for taking care of everything at practices and meets for the team. This included the same duties for away meets and championships, so I got to travel with the team.

Finally, the end of the school year had arrived, and my five-year journey at Andrew Lewis High School had come to an end. I graduated in the spring as a totally different person. From that first day of practice when I had gone out for football, I had reduced my weight from 317 pounds to 178 pounds. My waistline had gone from forty-nine inches to thirty-two inches.

More important than that was the "life-changing" transformation of my mental toughness, which would serve me well as I entered adulthood.

The Beginning of Adulthood

It was June 1960, and I was facing a "super life changer."

Andrew Lewis High School was behind me, and on the horizon loomed college, employment, marriage, children, and whatever else comes with adulthood. Fortunately, all these things don't happen at the same time. I had to be realistic and be able to separate my "desires" from my "possibles." Almost all my friends were going off to college, which would fall in my "desires" column. However, it did not make the "possibles" since I had no money. Also, Billy had worked hard for several years, and it was my turn now.

So that decision was made, and I began my job search. I saw an ad in the paper for jobs at a local furniture factory, Singer Furniture Company. I applied and was called by a recruiter to come to his office for an interview. He hired me immediately and instructed me to be at the factory the next day to begin work. When I arrived, there were crowds of people in the parking lots with signs. It was obvious that the employees were striking. It dawned on me that I was breaking through their lines to take away one of their jobs. I needed the job and didn't have any other choice. A person who breaks a strike line is called a scab.

Oh well, I guess I had been called worse things. I worked my shift that day and each day thereafter. My job was not hard, just tedious and boring. I was on an assembly line screwing drawer guides on dust bottoms. Furniture with drawers require a small rail in the middle that a groove in the bottom can slide on so the drawer stays straight when opened or closed. All day long I stood at the line with stacks of forty or fifty drawer dust bottoms rolling up. An assembly line never stops, and there are supervisors who make sure it doesn't. One by one I would place the drawer guide on and attach it with a screw using an air-powered drill which hung from a line above my head.

The strike lasted about a month, and the strikers returned. They had not forgotten that I was a "scab," and they let me know it. I was cussed and threatened everywhere I went. During work hours, they would shoot me with staple guns. I ignored them and didn't let it bother me. Eventually, some of the women I worked near decided I was an okay guy and left me alone. It was not long after that the harassment ended. I continued to work at the Singer Furniture Plant for a year. I had been able to make some money to help out at home. However, I knew that I needed to pursue better opportunities, and I was determined to do so. There were several options available to me. It was time to resign from my job and put together a plan.

CHRISTMAS ALONE

It was about this time that both Billy and I decided we were going to change our names slightly. Our father's name was Henry Preston Cecil, and Billy's was William Preston Cecil. Our mother's maiden name was Mildred Garland, and mine was James Garland Cecil. Billy wanted to be called Bill, and I chose to be Jim. We have used those names ever since.

I still had hopes of going away to college, but I knew that was not going to happen anytime soon. However, I had saved some money during my time at Singer Furniture and was ready to put it to good use now. My plan was to enroll in classes at a local university or community college. Bill and I discussed it, and he agreed. I talked to the registrar at the University of Virginia Extension in Roanoke and enrolled for classes for the fall semester. It was back to the classroom for the time being. I would worry about continuing through the spring once the first semester ended. Everything went well, and I finished the first semester with excellent grades.

It was Christmas, and it looked like I might be celebrating alone. I had not kept up with my high school friends and some were not coming home from college for the holidays. Others were celebrating with their families or taking trips to be with other friends. Bill was away visiting with someone he had met.

What it came down to was, I had no parents, no friends, and no money. I was determined to celebrate the holiday. At no time did I feel sorry for myself as I kept a positive attitude.

I waited until Christmas Eve to get a tree. I found a man who had been selling trees, and he had a few left. Since he was getting ready to close, he offered to give me one that he was going to throw away. I took it home and realized that I had no ornaments and no lights. That problem was solved when I cut out different-shaped pieces of cardboard and covered them with Reynolds Wrap. They were then hung on the tree with bent paper clips. I had enough money to buy a few of my favorite foods from the grocery store. Also on this trip, I picked up a few small boxes they were getting ready to throw away. When I returned home, I got a few things out that were my most cherished possessions and put them in the boxes. They were then wrapped in some scraps of newspaper and placed under the tree. It had been a full day, so I went to bed early. The next morning, I was up early and excitedly rushed into the living room to see what Santa had left me. I put on an eight-track tape of some Christmas music, ate my "goodies," and admired my beautiful tree. It was one Christmas I have never forgotten.

LETTER FROM MY UNCLE

The holidays were now over, and it was time to plan my immediate future. I wanted to continue taking classes, but I also needed to work. I began searching the want ads in the newspapers. A trip to the UVA registrar's office produced a schedule of classes for the spring semester. My hopes were that I could work during the day and take two classes at night. The following day, I was sitting in the living room trying to pick out my class selections when I heard the mailman leave several letters in my box. It was the usual assortment of bills, advertisements, and request for donations. However, one "official-looking" letter caught my eye. When I opened it and began reading it, I had to sit down in disbelief. It was written in a business type of format and stated,

> To: James G. Cecil

> Congratulations, you have been selected to become a participate in the 1962 Military Draft. You are hereby ordered to report on Friday, January 5,1962 to the Carlton Terrace Building located at 27 Jefferson Street in Roanoke , Virginia. You must arrive at 7:00 AM for a physical exam to determine if you are healthy enough to enter military duty. Once you are cleared by the medical staff you will be notified and released to return home. In approximately two weeks you

will receive your orders informing you where and when you are to report for your basic training.

Robert S. McNamara
Secretary Of Defense

I sat there absorbing what I had just read. While I had always been patriotic and had admired those serving in the military, I did not desire wasting two years of my life in The US Army. But, as the old saying goes, "*Uncle Sam wants you!*" I arrived promptly for my physical exam on the date specified in the letter. My only hope of not being accepted for the draft was that I would fail to pass the examination. I did have several minor ailments which gave me a slim chance of that happening.

When I arrived, I was sent to a large open room with about a hundred young men sitting in rows of folding chairs. At the front of the room was an officer in uniform standing at a podium. To his left, there were tables set up where six more soldiers were seated. In front of each one of them was a small sign showing a sequence of letters of the alphabet, for example *A-E*.

All the draft candidates were carrying on conversations until the officer at the podium called the crowd to order and introduced himself as Lieutenant Michael Sowder. He was all business as he stated the following, "You all know why you are here today. I am going to explain the procedure that we will be following. Pay attention and remember what I am about to tell you because you will only hear it once. We have a lot to cover, and it will require hours to complete. There will not be time for us to answer any questions, so we will furnish you with all the information you will need. To my left are six sergeants who will be calling out your names one at a time. When you hear your name called, you will step forward and present some form of identification. You will then be given a packet of forms and directed to an examining room. After the medical staff completes your exam, you will return to this room and wait until you are called to the front to learn the results. You will then be able to return home. If you do not come forward when you are called, your file will be

66

placed at the end, and you will be the last ones called. Gentlemen, we have a lot to accomplish today, and how well you follow our instructions will determine how soon you get to leave."

Since my last name was started with a *C*, I did not have to wait too long when they started calling us to come up front. After showing my ID and receiving my paperwork, I was escorted to an exam room. Following my physical, I returned to my seat to wait for my fate. An hour later, I was summoned to the table in the front.

The sergeant handed me several papers and said, "Congratulations, you passed with flying colors. If I were you, I would go home and start packing."

He also informed me that in a few weeks, I would receive my orders in the mail. They would explain in detail when and where I would report for my basic training. The die was cast as to my life for the next two years.

SIX MONTHS INSTEAD
OF TWO YEARS

A few days after the physical exam, I received a phone call from an Army recruiter. The conversation went something like this:

"Hello!"

"I am calling to speak to James Cecil."

"Yes, I am James Cecil."

"My name is Sergeant Wallace. I am an Army recruiter in Roanoke, and your name was referred to me. The reason that I am calling you is to discuss your recent induction into the Army. How do you feel about serving in the military for at least two years?"

"Let me put it this way. I think it is great for some people, but not everyone. I am sure you must be making the Army your career, and I admire you for your service to our country. However, I will be honest when I tell you that I have no desire to be a member of any military force."

"Well, thank you for being honest with me. What would you say if I told you there is a way to serve only six months on active duty instead of two years?"

"I am listening."

"Here is how it works. Instead of enlisting in the 'regular Army,' you would enlist in the 'Army reserve.' You would go through basic training, or boot camp as some call it, at a base. Once you complete your basic training, you would then then be assigned to another base to finish out your six months of 'active duty.' After that you would be sent home to return to civilian life again. Your only requirements after that would be to attend reserve training at your unit's center one weekend each month and two weeks of summer camp at a military fort."

"Sounds like a good deal to me. How long do I have to attend these monthly meetings and summer camps?"

"Not long, only nine years. Remember, it's six months or two years of active duty. The choice is yours. I can handle everything for you if you choose the six months."

"All right, I have made my decision, sign me up for the reserves."

The first week of March, I was on a Greyhound bus headed to Fort Jackson, Columbia, South Carolina. It would be my home for the next thirteen weeks. When I arrived in Columbia, a military bus was waiting to transport incoming recruits to the base. Once there, we were taken to temporary barracks and informed that another group was finishing up their training which had been delayed. They were scheduled to complete their duties and ship out in three weeks. This meant that we would be placed on hold until then. During that time, they made sure we would be kept busy. We were fitted with our uniforms, had our heads shaved, received four different injections, cleaned our barracks, and "policed" the grounds (picked up cigarette butts and other trash).

The three weeks seemed like three months, and everyone was anxious to get started. However, as the old saying goes, "Be careful what you wish for." Every morning they got us up at five o'clock to go for our morning run. In the beginning it was only for a mile, but every other day they increased it until we were covering five miles. The degree of difficulty was increased by numerous hills which had to be climbed. We were trained by three drill sergeants and a second lieutenant. The lieutenant was a recent college graduate from the University of Georgia. More than likely he had been an ROTC student and was fulfilling a two-year commitment. He seemed to be an okay kind of guy, and he mostly left us alone. The sergeants were another story since their job was to make our lives miserable. In a way it was ironic—I was rid of my abusive father, but now I had two drill sergeants who enjoyed tormenting me. I quickly learned that the best way to get through this ordeal was to keep your mouth shut, be inconspicuous, don't volunteer for anything, and do as you are told.

The other thing that I accepted was that there was nowhere for me to go, so I would try to learn as much as possible. The Army taught me a lot of things, some were beneficial, many were not. They taught me how to throw a live hand grenade, how to shoot a rifle, how to dissect a man with a bayonet, and how it felt to take off a gas mask while sitting in a tear gas chamber. On the brighter side, I learned the value of discipline, teamwork, toughness, and being organized. The thirteen weeks of basic training came to an end, and I was satisfied with my performance. Before we left Fort Jackson, everyone was given their orders, informing them when and where they would report next. I opened my envelope and learned that my next assignment was Fort Campbell, Kentucky, located on the border separating Tennessee and Kentucky. I was familiar with this base and knew it was the home of the 101st Airborne Division (Air Assault), better known as "the Screaming Eagles." Jumping out of an airplane was not in my plans, but I would cross that bridge when I got there. They gave me a week before I had to report, so I headed home for some R&R (rest and relaxation).

FORT CAMPBELL

I enjoyed my few days of rest and relaxation at home, but it passed all too quickly. Another long, tiring trip on a Greyhound bus was the next thing on my agenda.

When I arrived in Clarksville, Tennessee, I grabbed something to eat and then took a cab to the base. After asking for directions, I located the office and the sergeant that I needed to report to. When I was discharged from Fort Jackson, they warned me about being assigned to an advance infantry unit. They told me if that happened, I would spend the rest of my active duty similar to boot camp. The training would be more intense and extremely difficult. They recommended that I let the staff at Fort Campbell know that I was in the Army reserves and should be assigned to an office position.

As it turned out, that was exactly what happened, so they sent me to have an interview with an engineer group. When I arrived at their offices, they told me they had an opening for a draftsman. I let them know that I had taken a mechanical drawing class in high school. They stated that they would like to test me with some of their current projects. After reviewing my work, they were pleased, and I had the job for the duration of my active duty. Even though I wore a uniform and had to adhere to military protocol, it almost seemed like a civilian lifestyle. I got up each morning, ate breakfast, and reported for work. My working hours were 8:00 AM to 5:00 PM Monday through Friday, except Wednesday when we had the afternoon off for R&R. We were free on weekends to leave the base and do whatever we desired.

Even though my primary objective was to complete my active duty and return home, I had an ideal situation at Fort Campbell. I was thankful for how things were turning out for me. What I didn't know was that there were dark clouds forming on the world scene that would affect not only me but our entire country. Allow me to explain by stating how certain factors developed on the world stage back in 1959.

At the end of World War II in 1945, the United States and the USSR (Union of Soviet Socialist Republics) were allies along with Great Britain and France in defeating the Axis Powers (Germany, Italy, and Japan). Although World War II was over, the United States and Russia (USSR) became enemies in a different type of war, the Cold War.

Russia was determined to take over and convert to communism as many countries in the world as they could. At the same time, the United States was equally determined to stop them. Let us fast-forward to 1959 when our neighbors to the south, Cuba, was led by a corrupt dictator, Sergeant Batista. There was much unrest when another Cuban, Fidel Castro, led a rebellion and seized control of the country. Castro converted Cuba to communism, and it became another Russian puppet state. Of course, our government quickly became aware that we now had a potential enemy only ninety miles south of Florida. Another way of putting it was that Russia was in our backyard and posed a military danger. Needless to say, our military was keeping a constant visual scrutiny on all activity in Cuba. In April 1961, a plan was devised by our leaders to invade Cuba with armed forces in hopes of overthrowing Castro. The invasion forces were made up of Anti-Castro Cubans who were trained in the United States. It was called the Bay of Pigs Invasion. Unfortunately, the invasion was a disaster and failed.

As a result of this botched military plan, Castro took drastic steps to protect his country. He feared another invasion, this time by American troops. In 1962 he agreed to allow the Russians to deploy nuclear missiles in Cuba. This was a threat that our country could not allow to happen. Neither our government nor the Russians would give in. Our two countries had reached a stalemate. We were on the brink of war with the possibility of every word or action lighting the fuse. This all occurred between October 16 to 28, 1962, and was called "the Cuban Missile Crisis."

Russian ships were in the Cuban harbor ready to unload and set up nuclear missile sites. President John F. Kennedy was trying to negotiate a settlement with Nikita Khrushchev, the Soviet premier, in hopes of avoiding war. At first it appeared that the United States would have to invade Cuba to protect itself, on October 27, Fort Campbell was on high alert. All leaves were canceled, and everyone off base were ordered back. We were informed that we would be the first to invade Cuba. All preparations were being made, and we had to be ready to leave immediately once we heard the word "*Go*." Airplanes were fueled and on the tarmac. The troops were assembled and in their barracks. We nervously sat on our bunks and waited. All personnel were dressed in combat fatigues with our equipment and weapons in our laps. We waited and waited and waited! At first, there was a lot of chatter, and then things suddenly became quiet as each soldier was lost in their own private thoughts.

After waiting for several hours, our company commander burst through the door, and we all snapped to attention. He just stood there and looked at us for a minute.

He then said, "At ease, gentlemen. We have gotten some news. The president has reached an agreement with the Russians, and there will be no invasion. We don't have all the information yet, but it appears that he somehow has persuaded them to remove all their missiles."

A loud chorus of cheering from the troops filled the room along with a giant sigh of relief. As we learned later, President Kennedy had agreed to remove our missiles from Turkey if Russia would remove theirs from Cuba. I tried not to think about what could have happened. I guess, as they say, "I and the other troops dodged a bullet."

I want to state right now that I hold the highest regard for anyone who serves or has served in the military services. My father had his problems, but I was always proud of his bravery in combat for his country during World War II.

The rest of my active duty went by quickly and without incident. After being discharged, I packed up and again boarded a Greyhound for the long trip home. As I inhaled the smell of the diesel fumes and listened to the passengers' snoring, I began to put together a plan for the rest of my life.

EMPLOYMENT HISTORY

My first challenge was to find a job which would pay me a decent salary and fit in my busy schedule. I knew several people that worked at VDOT. After getting in touch with them, I was called in for an interview in January of 1963 and was hired on the spot. The job was a position on a survey party in Salem, and I worked there approximately a year.

When I learned that a private surveying firm, Dick and Wall, had an opening, I applied and decided to make a change. Both this and the one with VDOT were outside work which I enjoyed. However, on days when it was either extremely hot or the temperature was frigid, you would suffer. My surveying career lasted two more years and ended when I left to work in another profession in 1966.

My next endeavor was selling teeth for a company named Powers and Anderson Dental Supplies in Roanoke. Actually, my responsibilities were much more than just selling teeth. The company sold any and all kinds of dental equipment and supplies for dentist and dental labs. My title was "inside salesman," and I filled orders, managed inventory, answered the phone, and sometimes made deliveries if they were local. Again this job lasted a little over two years.

In 1968 a much better job with more responsibility and better pay presented a fortunate opportunity for me. My new employer was Sherwin Williams Paint Company. Sherwin Williams was a national leader in the paint industry with stores located in every state. As it turned out, this particular position was at a store located in Christiansburg, Virginia, so I had to move there. My title was "assistant branch manager" and "credit manager." In addition to paint we sold wallpaper, carpet, and a variety of tools. I was in charge of the branch anytime the manager was not present. It was a great deal of responsibility and my first experience as a collector. Collecting was an art that I quickly learned and turned into a successful career for many years. I had worked at the Christiansburg store for six months when one day our district manager paid us a visit. He called me aside and complimented me on my job performance. He then told me he wanted to promote me if I would agree to transfer to our branch in South Boston, Virginia. South Boston was a small rural town near the North Carolina border. He explained that if I accepted, there would be a nice salary increase. I gave it a lot of consideration and accepted the offer.

After I had rented an apartment and moved in, I used my time off from work to become familiar with the town and those who lived there. The countryside was mostly rural, and the people were extremely friendly. If you were driving down a country road and you passed someone working in a field, they would look up and wave to you. The branch manager was a great guy to work with. However, I was single, and there was not much to do. I had left behind a girlfriend, and on Saturdays when I was off, I would drive back to Roanoke. It did not take long for me to figure out that I needed to make a change. I contacted the district manager, explained to him how I felt, and asked for a transfer. He said he would let me know if an opening came up. A few weeks later, he called me and let me know they had a position open in Radford, Virginia. It was not in Salem or Roanoke but was only about an hour's drive away. The jobs in both South Boston and Radford were the same as I had in Christiansburg, a combination of assistant manager and credit manager. I accepted the transfer and made the move to Radford.

I spent two exciting years there. It afforded me the opportunity to rent an apartment three blocks from Radford College, which was a popular all-girls school. It is now Radford University and is coed. I worked hard and continued to impress my superiors. As it turned out, I had one more promotion and another move to make. I was promoted to central credit manager over all the stores in the Roanoke area. Up to that point, I had managed to not only advance in position but also increase my income and relocate to my home. I stayed with Sherwin Williams for five years, but decided to make a change in 1973.

The next stop on my road of employers was the largest furniture store chain in the South, Haverty Furniture Company, where I served as both a credit manager and office manager. I worked for Havertys for two years until 1975.

I left Havertys to start a totally different career with IDS (Investors Diversified Services), which at the time was the largest investment company in the world. In this job I held several insurance licenses as well as a national securities dealer license. In this position I sold life insurance, disability insurance, bonds, and mutual funds. I really enjoyed meeting and serving clients with their financial needs. However, the income was inconsistent from month to month.

In 1978 I had the opportunity to launch a career in banking, which lasted nineteen years. During my career I worked for five different banks and held the following positions: consumer loan officer, commercial loan officer, credit department manager, dealer floor plan auditor, credit analysis, bankruptcy department manager, charged off loan collector, manager of repossessed and impounded vehicles portfolio, and bank assistant vice president.

Toward the end of my banking career, large banks were constantly acquiring smaller banks in order to grow and expand to other markets. The last bank I worked for, First Union, had their main offices in Charlotte, North Carolina. They were involved in "takeovers" of several banks. In most of these mergers, the larger bank would have to meet certain concessions. This usually meant that the smaller bank would retain their employees. It also meant that some employees of the larger bank would either accept transfers or find other employment. The first time, First Union found me a job in the building where I worked. The second time, I decided that it was time for me to make a change.

In November 1997, I went to work for a nonprofit company, CCCS (Consumer Credit Counseling Service), in Roanoke. I successfully passed a three-hour exam to obtain a certified credit counseling license. In addition to two offices in Roanoke, they also had offices in Lynchburg, Martinsville, and Christiansburg. Clients would make appointments to come in for debt counseling and have some of their debts on a budget plan. Counselors were also required to conduct classes for first-time home buyers and budget classes. I found this work to be extremely gratifying since it involved helping people who were having financial problems. Actually, it was ironic that I was now helping people to pay their debts instead of collecting from them. I worked for CCCS for five years, from November 1997 to July 2002.

I began my last job in July 2002 and worked until October 13, 2013, when I retired. During a lot of my life, I was working a part-time job in addition to my full-time employment. I also was attending school at night at the University of Virginia Extension, Roanoke College, and Virginia Western Community College. When you add voluntary and public service commitments to all this, you can see that I stayed busy.

The next chapter will deal with these extra jobs and activities. After that, I will devote an entire chapter to my University of Virginia experience.

PART-TIME JOBS

During most of my life after I graduated from high school, I worked part-time jobs in addition to my full-time employment. Actually, I worked a part-time job as a boy. I had several newspaper routes. As far as working two jobs, I managed to do this several ways. One way was to work eight hours a day, from 9:00 AM until 5:00 PM, and then report to my part time job at 6:00 PM and work until 10:00 PM (or 11:00 PM). Another schedule would be to work the part-time job on weekends. The following is a list of part-time jobs and a description of each one:

- Sidney's—night manager of a popular women's clothing store in the Tanglewood Mall in Roanoke. This was one of eighty-one stores. I managed a staff of salesladies and balanced the day's books after closing.
- 7-Eleven convenience store—operated store during evening hours. I was responsible for waiting on all customers, stocking shelves, cleaning the store, ringing up sales, and anything else that needed attention.
- K-Mart Sporting Goods—handled operation of sporting goods department (this department was a separate department from the K-Mart store). The store normally closed at 10:00 PM but sometimes stayed open later. One Christmas Eve, when I was working, the store was still full of customers at 10:00 PM, so an announcement was made over the intercom: "Dear customers, our normal closing time is ten o'clock. Since it is Christmas, we are going to extend closing tonight to eleven o'clock." When 11:00 PM came,

they made the same announcement, except this time closing would be twelve o'clock. It was good for the customers and for K-Mart, but not so good for the employees who were planning to celebrate Christmas with their families.

- Census taker for 1970 Census—I worked at gathering data for United States Census Bureau. This information was obtained by the census taker visiting each address and interviewing the residents face-to-face. It required a lot of walking and knocking on people's doors.

- Kroger—this was not only a "part-time job" but an "only job" when I was a high school student. Toward the end of the summer, I took a job as a bag boy at the Kroger store in Salem. As it turned out, it was probably the shortest career in history. I began my "Kroger career" on a Saturday. Back in those days, every customer had their groceries bagged and then carried out to their car. On my first day on the job, I bagged a lady's groceries. The bags back then were brown paper, and some people liked to use a cardboard box. She had a purchased a lot of items; some of which were heavy. I got everything in her box and followed her to the car. When we got there, even though the box was heavy, I managed to lift it into the trunk. She looked at me and said, "When I get home, who is going to carry that box into my house?" I apologized and went back inside to get a few more boxes and bags. She seemed satisfied even though she never said anything when she left. I finished the day and checked out my schedule for the following week. It showed me working all day on Monday. I went to the store manager and explained to him, "I am sorry, but I can't come in to work on Monday." He replied, "Why is that?" "I have football practice," I answered. "So you are playing football? I need my employees to be here when I tell them. You will have to decide if you want to work for Kroger or you want to play football." I thought about it for two or three seconds and answered, "I will be playing football."

- Mowed grass at three bank branches—after I had been a bank manager for a few months, I noticed that the grass at my branch was not getting mowed frequently. Since the appearance of the building and the landscape were important, I complained to the vice president. He asked me if I wanted to mow it, and I asked him if he wanted to pay me. To my surprise he agreed, but only if I would also mow two other branches. We reached an agreement, and the "Jim Cecil Mowing Service" was in business. After that I occasionally mowed several other yards and lots for people.

- Quality Inn Motel auditor—in this job I was a night auditor at the Quality Inn on Interstate 81 in Salem, Virginia. It was my job to balance the books for both the motel and the restaurant. My hours were from 11:00 PM to 7:00 AM on weekends and holidays. I also was responsible for checking in late guests at the front desk during the night. It did not take long for me to learn that there were a lot of strange and dangerous things going on in the middle of the night, especially since I was the only employee there.

- The Family Golf Center—this was a golf driving range and pro shop in Roanoke. I worked there nights, weekends, and holidays. The manager and the owner had invented an interesting golf game. You could play a round of golf at the driving range instead of playing on a regulation golf course. The range was set up with different distances for driving from the tees and then making approach shots. There was a putting green to finish each hole. The pro shop sold everything a golfer would need, including clothing, shoes, clubs, balls, and golf bags.

VOLUNTEER INVOLVEMENTS

All my life, in addition to working two jobs and trying to earn a college degree, I have enjoyed being involved in volunteer endeavors.

According to Wikipedia, "Volunteering is generally considered an altruistic activity where an individual or group provides services, for no financial or social gain to benefit, for another group or organization."

The following are some of my volunteer involvements:

THE ROANOKE JAYCEES

When I was working at Haverty Furniture Store in downtown Roanoke, it was my responsibility to walk several blocks to a bank to make the store's deposit each day. The bank was First National Exchange Bank, and one day an employee approached me and began a conversation. His name was Bev Fitzpatrick, and he invited me to join the Roanoke Jaycees. The best way I could describe their organization is to quote their website:

> The Virginia Junior Chamber is the premier leadership training and community involvement organization dedicated to fostering leadership skills and personal development through projects in a variety of areas for young men.

I agreed to join the club, and it stands out as being one of my "life-changing" events. Being in the Jaycees gave me an opportunity to meet and become friends with many other men who were advancing in their professional careers. I benefited from one practice, which was required of each member. It was called "Speak Up," and at each meeting at least two members were selected to come before everyone and make a short speech. You never knew when you were going to be called on, and you were given the topic at the last moment. After being called on several times, I was finally able to defeat my fear of public speaking. The club was involved with a number of worthwhile projects all aimed at making Roanoke the "Star City of the South." Bev came to me and asked me to join him as a cochairman of a large ecology project. I was honored and agreed to undertake the challenge. As it turned out, the project was highly successful and became the largest ecology project in Virginia at that time. I had the pleasure of doing radio interviews, TV appearances, and newspaper reports. One of the fun things I got to do was to create a cartoon character named "Ecology Man," which was a superhero that appeared in each edition of the Jaycees newsletter. In all honesty, Bev led the way and took me "under his wing." I finally had to leave the Jaycees because they had an age limit of thirty-five years. Once you reached your thirty-fifth birthday, you were considered to be an exhausted rooster." Even though I was no longer in the club, I continued to stay in touch with a lot of the members.

Bev and the entire Fitzpatrick family became my close friends who have stood behind me through the good and the bad times. I will always consider them to be my "second family." I owe Bev; his wife, Shirley; his two brothers, Eric and Broadus; and his children, BT and Abbi, my gratitude.

THE LIONS CLUBS

Shortly after I had begun my banking career, I joined the Tanglewood Breakfast Lions Club. The club was in the Tanglewood Mall area where my bank branch was located. After being active in this club for several years, I transferred my membership to the Vinton Lions Club. I was still with the bank but no longer in that area of town. My wife, Pat, was a high school teacher at William Byrd High School in Vinton, which was part of Roanoke County. We had bought a house there, so it made sense to join the Vinton Club. Again, I will quote from a Lions Club website:

> The Lions Club mission to empower volunteers to serve their communities, meet humanitarian needs, encourage peace and promote international understanding How are The Lions accomplishing their mission? In 1925 Helen Keller addressed the Lions Clubs International Convention in Cedar Point, Ohio, USA, and challenged the Lions to become "knights of the blind in the crusade against darkness."

Since then, the Lions have worked tirelessly to aid the blind and visually impaired. In 1990, through Sight First, Lions were restoring sight and preventing blindness on a global scale. They have raised more than $346 million for this initiative. Sight First targets the major causes of blindness: cataract, trachoma, river blindness, childhood blindness, diabetic retinopathy, and glaucoma. Lions collect and refurbish used eyeglasses for distribution. They also sponsor training schools for seeing eye dogs, which will be provided to the blind. In addition to Sight First, the Lions around the world are working to raise awareness, bring medical care, and provide education to help prevent hearing loss. More than 275 million people worldwide are hearing-impaired or deaf according to the World Health Organization. Lions formally identified hearing conservations as a major activity in the early 1970s.

They also fund programs for dogs to guide people with hearing impairments. These hearing guide dogs are trained to respond to household sounds like a knock on the door, a smoke alarm, or even a baby's cry. Another program was to collect old hearing aids, which were not being used, and refurbish them to be given to needy patients.

The Lions Clubs in Virginia were divided into districts, and the Vinton Club was in District 24E. The district governor asked me to be the district chairman for Hearing Conservation, and I accepted. One of the requirements for this position was to write a speech and present it to each of the fifty-two clubs in the district. My term was for a year, and I had to spend a lot of time and many miles of travel to accomplish my goal. I also tried to come up with some new ideas to collect more hearing aids. One idea I had was to attend a funeral directors' conference. I gave a presentation to them asking that when they received a body, to check and see if the deceased wore hearing aids. Since they no longer needed them, we would like to have them if the next of kin approved.

Also I had the privilege of visiting a department at the University of Virginia Medical Center which was developing a cochlear implant for the hearing-impaired. A cochlear implant is an electronic medical device that replaces the function of the damaged inner ear. Unlike hearing aids, which make sounds louder, cochlear implants do the work of damaged parts of the ear (cochlea) to provide sound signals to the brain.

Each Lions club could also at their discretion implement different projects or programs that were for the benefit of their local town or city. I was a member in two Lions' clubs over a span of twenty years. During that time, I served in various officer positions and was the club president two years consecutively in the Tanglewood Club and one year in the Vinton Club.

Some additional volunteer jobs, projects, and programs I was involved with are as follows:

- Homeless people—I served meals to homeless men and women in a Roanoke soup kitchen.
- City rescue mission—I served meals to poor and underprivileged families in Roanoke.
- Christmas party—I played Santa Clause at a party for sixty youngsters. They were treated to a movie with popcorn and soft drinks. Each one got to talk to "Santa," who gave them a nice present These children came from poverty-stricken families who otherwise would have no Christmas.

- Martha Jefferson Hospital—served as a concierge at one of the hospital's medical buildings in Charlottesville. Also filled in when necessary in the Cancer Care Center.
- Second Presbyterian Church—cotaught a Sunday school class for teens with Broaddus Fitzpatrick in Roanoke.

One of my most unique volunteering experiences that I became involved with occurred when I lived in Greensboro, North Carolina. I had an opportunity to play on a blind softball team in a sport called "BeepBall." Yes, I said *blind*.

In the spring of 1992, I accepted a banking position with a bank in Greensboro. As it turned out, I looked at the move as a temporary opportunity until I could get back with a bank in the Roanoke area. We kept our home in Vinton, and Pat and Anne stayed there. I rented a small apartment in Greensboro and came home on weekends. One day in May 1992, an article in *The News and Record* caught my eye. It was titled "Beepball: Greensboro's Entry in the Sport for the Blind Has Just about Been Unbeatable." With fascination I read about a group of young men who were legally blind. Most of them had been blind since birth and were employees of Industries of the Blind in Greensboro. The article stated that the team was looking for volunteers to help with practice and games.

Since I did not have anything to do in the afternoons, I gave them a call. They invited me to attend their next practice. After meeting the players and another volunteer, Kathy Shoffner, I was accepted as a member of the team. One of my responsibilities as a volunteer was to help with equipment at all games and practices.

I also played (blindfolded) in several games when we did not have enough players. I also drove their bus when we had an away game.

It was inspiring and uplifting to be around these men who lived their life in darkness. It was obvious they had accepted their disadvantage early and no longer considered it a handicap. I fulfilled my duties for two seasons with the team. During the second season, I was able to obtain a banking position back in Roanoke and moved back home.

On the following pages, you will find the newspaper article and a few pictures of the team players.

Beepball: Greensboro's entry in the sport for the blind has just about been unbeatable

● Greensboro's Beepball team (players legally blind) has not lost a game in three years — and is aiming for bigger things.

BY LISA D. MICKEY
Staff Writer

There have been games when they knocked the *beep* out of the ball.

Literally.

In such games, Greensboro's Beepball team, which plays the brand of softball designed for the visually impaired, slugged the beeping mechanism right out of the center of the ball.

Greensboro's team is such a force in the sport that it has won the last four North Carolina/South Carolina state tournaments and hasn't lost a game in three years. The team also has won 9 of 14 tournaments played in this region.

"Everybody's after us," said player-coach Glenn Permar, 38, a member of the Greensboro team for almost 20 years.

In the second round of last year's double-elimination state beepball tournament, Greensboro was beating Charlotte 33-12 in the third inning when Charlotte's frustrated players gave up and walked off the field.

But as luck would have it, Charlotte ended up facing Greensboro again in the championship. Greensboro won that game 59-23.

Just because all but two of the team's 12 members are completely blind, don't think their commitment to the sport or their competitive fire is any less than that of sighted players.

In games and practices, the players dive to the ground in an effort to stop the beeping ball, thereby preventing the other team from scoring once the ball is in the possession of the defensive field player.

They also waste no time in charging to one of the two beeping bases when they hit a pitch. The object is to score a run by reaching the beeping base before the defensive player has possession of the ball.

Beepball players are athletes who risk injury to play the game. Collisions are common, as well as scrapes and breaks from having to play on poor quality athletic fields. On one such field in Durham last

his ankle on the rocky surface, while a Raleigh player broke his arm.

But Greensboro's team has remained undaunted to hardships through the years. Thanks to a $4,500 gift from the Greensboro Jaycees, they have already raised $6,000 of the $9,000 they need to compete in the Beepball World Series in Minneapolis Aug. 18-23.

They believe that going to the World Series in their sport would be the ultimate proving ground. It will be the first time a team from the Carolinas has competed in the 20-team double-elimination event.

"We've talked about it for years," said Permar. "It's a big thing and we really don't know what to expect. But we think we would do OK."

Greensboro's Beepball team was formed in 1972 with the help of the Telephone Pioneers of America, who helped devise the game in 1964. The local team is still sponsored by the Communication Workers of America (CWA) Post 3607, which sends the squad to the state tournament each year.

Greensboro was one of the first beepball teams to organize on the East Coast, aside from Florida. For many years, their closest geographic competitors were located in Illinois.

Then teams formed in Charlotte, Winston-Salem, Spartanburg, S.C., Raleigh, High Point and Durham. New teams are now forming in Thomasville, Columbia, S.C. and Charleston, S.C., with this year's state tourney in Charleston Aug. 14-15.

In a typical beepball game, each team has a sighted pitcher and catcher, as well as one to two sighted spotters on the field. Game fields are divided into seven pie-shaped sections, with five defensive players positioned across the field.

The catcher establishes a target area for the pitcher and the pitcher attempts to consistently pitch to the target from a distance of 20 feet.

Batters are given five pitches, four of which may be strikes. Once the ball is hit, the spotters inform the infield which section of the field the ball is likely to land.

"I've been volunteering with the team off and on for 16 years," said Kathy Shoffner, who serves as an umpire, spotter and team van driver. "I enjoy watching this more than a regular baseball game."

no small feat. Greensboro's beepball team played exhibitions with the Atlanta Braves baseball team for three years and only once did a sighted, but blindfolded pro player hit the ball.

"You have to have a rhythm to it," said Robert Crandell, 27, who has played beepball since the seventh grade. "When the pitcher throws the ball, I count about three seconds before I swing. Nine out of 10 times, I'll hit it."

Interestingly, Greensboro has the only legally blind pitcher in the entire N.C./S.C. Beepball Association. Lonnie Cunningham was a regular field player when the team's sighted pitcher quit coming to beepball games.

"We tried and tried to recruit volunteers," Permar said. "Finally, Lonnie said he would try pitching for us."

Cunningham lost the first game he pitched by a run, but is 40-0 since.

Crandell and one other player are blindfolded when they compete because they have some degree of vision. Beepball players must be legally blind to compete.

All but two of the players work at the Industries of the Blind in Greensboro. Most of the team members have been playing beepball together for years.

"Everybody's determined to win," said Permar. "We're out there together."

The team also is determined to survive. They are constantly looking for volunteers and funding is a consideration during the team's summer season. They typically play twice a month May through July, with the state and World Series tournaments scheduled in August.

Aside from funds to travel to tournaments, the team goes through 20 of the 16-inch beeping balls a year, which cost $25 each.

"We always welcome volunteers and sponsors," Permar said. "And, we hope that if we go to the World Series and do well, it'll become an annual thing."

For more information about the Greensboro Beepball Team, call Glenn Permar at 292-1401 or Kathy Shoffner at 273-3548. The team practices at 6:30 p.m. each Wednesday on a field behind the football stadium on the N.C. A&T State University campus. Their first home game will be held June 13 at Old Peck softball field on Glenwood Avenue.

JIM CECIL

Some Pets That I Have Owned

After I had graduated from high school, there were several pets that I remember fondly. I have always loved animals, and over the years I owned a variety of them, some normal and some weird. Here is a short list of the most memorable ones:

Iguana

I decided that I would enjoy owning an iguana, so I bought one from a pet store in Roanoke. At the time I was living in an apartment, and I put out water and food for it. It was allowed to roam free, and it loved to hang on the drapes. One day I received a phone call from a gentleman who asked me if he could come over to talk about insurance. I agreed, and he showed up that night right on time. We sat down on my sofa, and he spread out two notebooks on a coffee table. They contained all kinds of statistics and other data which were supposed to convince me to purchase several types of insurance. My iguana was large and ugly. I noticed when we sat down that he was hanging on a drape across the room. Mr. Insurance Salesman was just getting into his sales pitch and pointing to the illustrations and charts in his books. He suddenly stopped talking, and when I glanced at him, he had this look of fear on his face. He was just sitting there with eyes locked on the iguana. Suddenly, in a panic, he jumped up from the sofa, grabbed his notebooks, and headed for the door. As he scurried across the room, he shouted, "I just remembered I have another appointment that I am late for." I never saw or heard from him again. My iguana lived for about a year, but when winter came, he could not adapt to the cold, and he eventually died.

TARANTULA

My next purchase from the pet store was a big, hairy tarantula. Unlike the iguana, it was not allowed to be out of a large aquarium tank. It really did not have much of a personality and just sat there in its glass house and occasionally moved around. I fed it grub worms, and it seemed happy enough. It was about the size of my hand, and I enjoyed bringing girls to my apartment and inviting them to see the "fish" in the aquarium tank. I never figured out why most of my dates were a onetime thing only. I had paid ten dollars for my spider, and I decided that I was better off without him. Maybe if I got rid of him, I would have a better chance at a second date. Oh well, maybe the spider was not the problem; perhaps it was me they did not like. Regardless, the pet shop owner bought it back for ten dollars, and everyone was happy.

PIRANHA

I had a lot of people tell me that I should get some fish for the aquarium tank. So I took their advice and bought a piranha. Here is a description of this fish if you are not familiar with it. It is a ferocious schooling, freshwater fish and is six to ten inches in length. Piranhas are native to warm rainforest lowland streams and lakes in South America—the Amazon basin. They are known for their sharp teeth and aggressive appetite for meat. They have a single row of teeth in both jaws. Their teeth are tightly packed and interlocking and used for rapid puncture and shearing. Piranhas are flesh-eating fish which are attracted to blood. When I brought mine home, I had to figure out what to feed it. The first thing I tried was some raw hamburger meat. It circled around and appeared to be in an attack mode. However, it never ate the meat, so I had to go to plan B. I decided that it was only going to eat something that was alive, so I went to a local bait shop and bought some minnows. I dropped a few in the tank and watched to see what it would do. It swam near the minnows, made a few circles, and then attacked. The slaughter took only a few seconds, and the only thing left in the tank was the piranha. I continued to use the minnows until one day the bait shop stopped selling them. It was in the fall and there was no demand for them since the weather had turned cold. That was when I paid a visit to a store that had a pet department. They had some nice, fat goldfish, so I bought a few, and the problem was solved. One day after I had fed my fish, I noticed one of the goldfish's head was lying on the bottom of the tank. I had a little hand net that was made to catch fish in aquariums. Without thinking, I reached in the water to pick up the severed head with the net. The piranha dived in a flash as I jerked my hand out of the water. When I examined the net, I found that the bottom was completely gone. The next thing I did was to be sure I still had all my fingers. They were all still there, but a lesson had been learned. One day when I went to the store to buy his food, the salesman asked me what I was doing with all the goldfish he was selling me.

When I didn't answer him, he said, "You are feeding them to a piranha, aren't you? Don't come back here again."

Fortunately, spring arrived, and I was able to get some minnows again. I kept the piranha for a long time, but one morning I found it floating motionless at the top of the water. It had eaten its last meal.

JAMBALAYA

In one of my bank jobs, I worked at a large regional operation center. From time to time I had a small aquarium at my desk. I found it extremely relaxing to see the colorful fish swim around all day. One day when I did not have any fish in the tank, an employee told me she had caught a crawfish (or crayfish) in a creek. She offered to give it to me if I wanted it. She brought it in the next day, and I set up its new home in the aquarium. I named it Jambalaya. I did some research on the internet to see what crawfish eat. I was surprised to discover that they eat lettuce, small pieces of vegetables, and fish pellets. Jambalaya seemed to be enjoying his new home, but after a week, I noticed an interesting game he seemed to be playing. The bottom of the tank was lined with tiny, colorful rocks which a lot of people have in their aquariums. In the morning he would pick up one of the rocks with his claws and carry it to the other side of the tank. He would then return, pick up another one, and carry it to the other side. He would repeat this activity all day long until he had a nice, high mound. I found this exercise to be fascinating, so at the end of the day before I left work, I reached in the tank and pushed all the rocks back to the original side. Of course, he spent every day relocating them every time I moved them. I kept him for a long time and finally gave him back to the lady who had given him to me. She let me know she had put him back in the creek where she had found him. So if you are out hiking, and you find a creek with all the rocks piled on one side, be sure to tell Jambalaya that I miss him.

One Dog and Two Cats

Buck

After the demise of the piranha, I decided to stick to a more conventional pet. I obtained a dog which I named Buck. He was not a pedigree, just a plain old mongrel. He was big and strong and well-known around Salem. Around the time that I had Buck rock and roll, fast cars, and "cruising" were the things everyone spent their time doing. The two most popular drive in restaurants in Salem were Lendy's and Yoda's. These were the days when you pulled up to a parking space and called your order in over a call box and the carhop would bring your food out to the car. The plan for the night was always the same. First of all, you spent all day washing, waxing, and getting your car ready for the evening. Then you showed off your "wheels" by driving through one of the two restaurants. If you didn't see anyone you knew, you would drive over to the other restaurant and do the same thing. You repeated this over and over, again and again. Although the two restaurants were only ten miles apart, you might drive a hundred miles in an evening. A lot of times I would take Buck with me, and he would sit in the front with his head out the window. As I made several laps around the parking lot, people would wave and yell, "Hey, Buck, there is Buck, the wonder dog!" The thing that bothered me was that I did not know them, but they knew Buck. We had to keep an eye on him, or he would go off on his own and get into a lot of trouble. He spent a good deal of time in the house, and he seemed to have the idea that he was allowing us to stay with him and he was the boss. He had some bad habits which at times could be disgusting. For example (I don't want to be crude), he would lie in the floor and pass gas. He would then look up at each of us as if to ask, "Which one of you did that?" He also for some reason lay across doorways and refused to let anyone by. When he was outside, we had to put him on a long chain attached to a tree. Of course, he was able to get loose and run all over Salem until we could find him. One day when I was home a good friend of mine, Donnie Butler, visited me.

He asked me, "Where is Buck?"

"He is in the backyard," I replied.

Donnie laughed. "I don't think so. I just saw him run through a red light at the intersection up the street."

So it was time to go Buck hunting again. We eventually found him, but every time we got close, he would take off running away.

I could almost see the joy in his face as we helplessly played a version of "dog tag" and he was winning. We finally decided to just keep the car moving until he got worn out. He kept pace with us for a while, but then we could see him fading. He finally ran out of gas before we did, and he came up and jumped in the car. Another day he disappeared from the backyard, and I received a call from a man who did not identify himself. He informed me that Buck was playing around on the courthouse lawn in the middle of Salem and asked me to come up and get him. The house that Bill and I were renting was across the street from the Roanoke River. Buck loved to wade out to a shallow part of the river and catch fish in his mouth, much like the grizzly bears in Alaska catch salmon and trout. However, there are no trout or salmon in the Roanoke River, just carp.

The house that Bill and I were renting, where His Royal Highness Buck the Wonder Dog reigned supreme, had a large front porch. A long hallway led through the interior of the house. The front door was rather ornate, and the center was completely glass. One day I was in the tub taking a bath, and Buck was lying in a doorway enjoying his afternoon nap. Everything was quiet and peaceful until the doorbell rang. The next thing I heard were Buck's toenails clicking on the hardwood floors, followed by loud barking, growling, and snarling. There was not much I could do except soak in the tub and wait to see how this was going to work out. I didn't have to wait long, and the results were not good. In this sequence of events, I heard the following: Buck hitting the front door, a loud shattering of glass, a man's scream, the sound of a person running off the porch, and finally silence. I just lay in the tub trying to visualize all this and what I would find when I got up. As I lay there, someone or something pushed the partially closed bathroom door open. It was His Majesty, and the first thing that came to mind was, "Wonder Dog," the only "wonder" was that I wondered why I kept him. I would have to admit he looked so pitiful. He looked sadly at me as he raised his right paw up. It appeared to have a deep cut, and the blood was dripping on the floor. I got out of the tub, dried off, and bandaged his wound.

Next, I went to see if we still had a front door. The wooden framework was intact, but there was no longer any glass. Broken glass was everywhere on the front porch, but not in the house. Buck must have hit the door with such force the glass shattered outward. There was also a small bag lying on the porch. I picked it up and examined the contents; it contained a prescription from a drugstore for Bill. Back in those days you could call in prescriptions and the drugstore would deliver them. I could imagine that the poor guy who delivered this one probably needed some mental therapy. Eventually, I called the drugstore and apologized, Buck's wound healed, I cleaned up the mess, and the door was replaced. It is always painful when an owner loses their pet, and I can only compare it to losing a family member or a close friend. I had to move and could not continue to keep Buck, so he went to live with a girlfriend I had been seeing. That relationship turned out to have inconsolable deficiencies and sadly ended. After that I did not have any further contact with her, so I never knew what happened to Buck.

TAFFI

I had no pets for a long time after Buck. Instead I had a wife, Pat, and a daughter, Anne. We bought our first home in a subdivision in Vinton, Virginia. After living there for several years, I informed Pat that I wanted to adopt a small kitten. She agreed, and I checked ads in the newspaper. I found one a lady in Roanoke had posted. It stated she had a cat that had a litter of kittens, and she wanted to find a home for them. We drove over to her house and took a look at them. She had them together in a large cardboard box. Before I could look at them, I noticed a small hole in one side of the box. Suddenly this little head stuck out of it, and its eyes rested on me. I couldn't resist; I had found my kitten. A famous poet, Ogden Nash, once said, "The trouble with a kitten is that eventually it becomes a cat."

I named him Taffi, and he turned out to be an amazing animal. He had two qualities that were almost mind-boggling. He was extremely intelligent, and he actually did have nine lives. If Buck was "wonder dog," Taffi was "super cat." I will give you several examples as to why I determined that he was smarter than most cats.

We lived in a subdivision on a block that had three houses. Our street in the front of our home was the Main Street through the subdivision, so it had a lot of traffic. There was a street on each side of our block that ran at a right angle away from the back of our house. Taffi spent most of his days outside and was free to go anywhere he wanted. We had set up a small area in the basement which we called his apartment. At nights he would come in after dark and go to his room. He never used a litter box, but he always let us know when he needed to go outside. He made friends with a black cat that lived next door and another cat that lived up the street behind us. Each morning he would go outside jump over our chain-link fence in the back and head up to the house behind us. The people that lived there told us he would walk up the stairs behind their home and wait until their cat would come out. They would play most of the day like a couple of kids.

He also became "buddies" with the cat next door. We had a front porch across the front of our home where I enjoyed sitting and watching the cars drive by. A lot of times Taffi would show up and either sit or lie down beside me. I noticed that, just like me, he kept his eyes on the vehicle until it had passed. We had some friends who lived on the same street as his cat playmate. They lived further up the street, and it was not a short walk. I would ask him if he wanted to go for a walk, and as I started up the street, he followed me. He walked by my side all the way to our neighbor's house, much like a dog would. When we got there, I would go inside and he lay down in the front yard. No matter how long I visited, I always found him waiting for me when it was time to walk back.

Taffi had some "accidents" and "ailments" from time to time, and it was necessary to give him medications. One time he got into a fight with another cat and sustained a small wound. The vet gave me antibiotic pills to give him. The method of giving an animal a pill is to make him sit still, open his mouth, insert the pill, and rub his throat until he swallows. It sounds simple (or maybe not), so I picked him up and set him on a laundry dryer that was in the basement. As he calmly sat there, I was feeling good about the first step. With confidence I opened his mouth and inserted the pill. All that remained was to rub his throat to send the medication down. To my amazement he continued to sit there without making a move. I waited a few minutes to be sure the pill was in his stomach. Satisfied with my ability to complete the entire procedure without a problem, I turned to take a step away. That is when I heard a ping that sounded like something small had hit the top of the metal dryer. Of course, Taffi was still just sitting there, and in front of him was the pill. I scolded him and informed him that we were going to try this all over again. We went through the same plan a second time with the same result. On the third try, I thought we had accomplished our mission since I had not heard the ping. I felt even better when I could not find the pill on the dryer. However, when I picked him up, I found the pill lying under his paw. He had deliberately leaned down, spit the pill out, and covered it. I had to admire his cunning, and I rewarded him by simply giving up hope of giving him the medicine. It would be up to him to heal his wound, which he did.

Taffi was not only smart; he was extremely resilient. He convinced me that some cats do have nine lives. The first evidence of this happened one day when he got hit by a car. A Volkswagen Beetle's front tire grazed him and knocked him over. When I examined him, I found an impression of the car's right front tire tread imprinted on his side. A trip to the veterinarian's confirmed that he had no external or internal injuries. Another time he decided it would be a lot of fun to climb to the top of a tall tree in the backyard. Getting up there was not a problem, but getting down was another matter. He slipped and lost his balance, plummeting forty feet to the ground. He hit the grass on his feet with no indication of any pain or injury. Apparently, all his cat neighbors were not his friends. He quite frequently came home with battle wounds from encounters with felines who had bad attitudes.

Taffi always seemed to heal and come back strong. However, his toughest challenges were yet to come. He would spend his days outside but would always come in the house after dark.

One night he did not show up, and I went outside and called him. He did not come, but the black cat that lived next door showed up. He walked up and kept meowing and turning away. All of a sudden, I realized he was trying to get me to follow him. We walked over near a rail fence that ran down the side of our yard, and there lay Taffi on his side, not moving. I picked him up and headed for the house. It was dark, but when I got to the porch, I noticed that I had blood all over my hands. He was bleeding on his side. It was obvious that he had somehow been injured. I took him into the house, cleaned him up, and managed to temporarily stop the bleeding. The next morning we rushed him to the vets as soon as they opened. They kept him all day and called us that evening to let us know what had happened and how he was doing. We were shocked at what we learned. Someone had shot him with a rifle, and they had to remove a pellet type of bullet. We were told that he would survive and that we could come in to see him the next day. When we arrived for our visit, we found one of the most pitiful sights that I have ever seen. Poor Taffi was unconscious, lying on his back, with IVs in his legs. They had shaved him from his chin to his rear end, and he had stiches the entire length of his stomach. It took a while, but he did survive and eventually healed completely.

Unfortunately, this was just the first chapter in this saga. Almost exactly a year later, he was shot again. This time the bullet missed his vital organs, and the vet informed us that surgery would not be necessary. His body would heal around the projectile once the healing was complete. They released him to go home but instructed us to not let him go outside for a few weeks. We followed their advice, and he finally regained his freedom. Everything went fine for another couple of weeks, when to our dismay, he was shot a third time. After taking him back to the vets, we asked some of our friends if they had seen anyone shooting a rifle or pistol in the neighborhood. What we found out was interesting. We were told that there had been several instances of a lady shooting a rifle from her patio. One time she almost hit some children who were playing in a backyard near her house. She lived on a street which ran off our road in a house which was about a half block away. We decided it was time to get the police involved, so we contacted the county sheriff's department. They sent out a deputy, who was courteous and helpful. He listened to the entire history of the three shootings but exclaimed he could not do anything unless he knew who the shooter was. We told him what we had learned from our neighbors about the lady up the street. He said he would go to her house but he was sure she would deny everything. He left, and we waited to see what he was able to find out. We did not have to wait long, and this was the result.

He found her in her driveway washing her car. He informed us that their conversation went as follows:

"I am with the Roanoke County Sheriff's Department."

"Why are you here, what do you want?"

"I need to ask you some questions. Do you know the Cecils who live down the street?"

"Yes, I know who they are."

"Someone has been shooting their cat, do you know anything about that?"

"Yes, I know all about it, I am the one who shot him."

"All three times?"

"Yes, all three times."

When we heard this, we couldn't believe it. He continued by explaining to us what would happen next. She had been charged and would appear in court before a judge at a later date. The judge would hear the case, make a ruling, and determine a sentencing. The date of the trial arrived, and we were in attendance. She had hired an attorney, and we overheard him tell her, "This won't take long, I am going to get you off."

Unfortunately for her, that was not the case (no pun intended).

After she was called to the witness stand, the prosecuting attorney began his examination:

"Did you shoot the Cecils' cat?"

"No."

"You have already admitted that you did. What is your defense?"

"I didn't shoot him, I was trying to miss him in order to chase him away."

"Well then, you are a terrible shot because you hit him in the stomach every time."

The defense attorney tried to portray that the defendant was remorseful and should not be punished. However, the judge found her guilty and announced sentencing. She received one year in jail, was required to reimburse us for all the vet bills, which were several thousand dollars, and was fined $1,000. The jail sentence was changed to probation. She was advised that if anything further happened to Taffi within that year, the police would come to see her.

As for Taffi, he survived again, but he was starting to run out of lives. He managed to make it through another two years. One night he did not come in, and it was getting late. I went outside to look for him, and I found him lying on his side in the yard. I picked him up, but he did not move. *It was obvious that he was dead.* We had heard about a lady up the street that was known to have poisoned some cats. They had even found some cat carcass in her trash. He had no marks on him that would indicate he had been injured in any way. He might have been poisoned, or he might have died of old age. I would never know, and I didn't really care. All that I knew was that he was gone and I had lost my buddy, my companion, my best friend. That night I wrapped his body in a sheet and buried him in a grave in a flower bed in the backyard. I molded a concrete tombstone and etched his name on it.

INDY

It took me two years before I was ready to own another pet. I decided that I would like to have another cat, and we looked in the papers for someone who had kittens available for adoption. One day we found an ad, and we called the owner and got some information from her. She explained that she had a litter that were old enough for a new home. She described what that looked like and said that one of them was a blue cat. I told Pat that I had never seen a blue cat and if it was blue, I wanted it. When we arrived, she gathered up the kittens, and we could not believe our eyes. This cat was, indeed, a grayish blue color. We brought him home, but he apparently had been a "barn" cat. He had not been inside a house and was wild. He would not let us get near him even though we tried for a couple of days. He finally climbed up inside the motor of a freezer. We decided it would be the right thing to do if we returned him. We took him back to his home, but we did not pick out another one.

Several weeks went by, and I had decided to wait awhile before I resumed my search for a kitten. At the time I was working at a huge operation center for First Union Bank. One day a coworker came to me and asked me if I was still trying to adopt a cat. She said some of the employees who worked at a loading dock had found a stray kitten wandering around their area. They were afraid it might get run over by a truck. When I went down there to check it out, I found this tiny little kitten. It was so small it fit in the palm of my hand. The amazing thing was that it looked exactly like Taffi. Later, after it grew up, if you looked at a picture of it, you would not know which cat it was. It was almost as if it Taffi was reincarnated. Of course, I had to take it home. The next day was the Fourth of July, so I named it Indy in honor of Independence Day. He could not have been more than a few weeks old and seemed to be afraid at first.

We found out that if he saw or heard a plastic grocery bag, he shook with fear. I figured that some cruel person had put him and maybe other kittens in a similar bag and dumped them on the side of a road. After he was sure that I meant him no harm, he was an extremely lovable pet. I am convinced that he thought I was his mother and that I would protect and care for him. I used to sit in a La-Z-Boy recliner, and he would jump up and lay his head on my shoulder and put his paw around my neck. He would then take a long nap. He did have an annoying habit, which was snoring while he slept. We were living in Vinton at the time, but moved to Charlottesville seven years later. He had a problem at first with moving to our new home. Cats usually get set in their ways, and they don't like changes to their routines. However, he adjusted, and we kept him for another four years. I had been an insulin-dependent diabetic for about forty years. After one of Indy's visit to the vets, we were told that he also had diabetes and would require daily insulin injections. Each morning I would get up and give myself my insulin shot first and then his. To my surprise he knew exactly what I was going to do, but still held still and never flinched. His condition became worse, and eventually the vet informed me that there was nothing she could do to help him. He would go through days of suffering, so the humane thing to do was to put him to sleep. I gave her permission to proceed, and it was again time to mourn the loss of another pet. Indy was the last animal that I have owned.

SECOND INTERMISSION

Let us take a short break from the previous chapters of the journey of my life. I have given you a sample of the good and the bad, the happy and the sad. I tried to add a dose of humor along the way, and I hope you have enjoyed reading it. I emphasized those events that I considered were either "game changers" or "life changers."

However, in looking at the entire story, these early chapters should have a subtitle "Appetizers." Please believe me when I tell you, they pale in comparison to what you are about to read. Just as in the movies, I am going to give you a brief "preview." The remaining chapters will cover my life from 2001 to 2018. During this time period, you will learn how, with a lot of determination, I accomplished one of my lifelong goals. You will also find out how I survived while amassing over six hundred pages of medical records at one hospital.

Also, I am aware that in the previous pages, I have mentioned friends, close family members, relatives, etc. In the next chapter you will learn more about some of these important people in my life. It will be obvious how knowing them influenced me and made me a better person.

So Now the Remainder of My Journey Begins

2001

The year was 2001, and I had been working for Consumer Credit Counseling Service for four and a half years. During that time, I had seen it go from a nonprofit agency to charging a fee for their services. It was still a great deal for the clients. We got their interest rates reduced, managed their debts, helped them with budgeting and taught them free classes. I liked the work, and it was rewarding to be able to help clients who were in trouble financially. The small fee they had to pay did not bother me. However, we started doing telephone interviews. I and the other counselors had to alternate working late nights until 10:00 PM, and when we left work, we had to carry a cell phone. We might receive a call and have to do a one-hour interview anytime anywhere during the night. I didn't receive many calls during the middle of the night, but there were a few. They were usually someone who was either drunk or they were lonely and wanted someone to talk to. We also heard some rumors that the owners might be selling the business to a large company in Texas. I wasn't quite ready to jump ship just yet, but that was about to change.

I have always believed that our lives are what we make of them. Other people are convinced that our destiny is controlled by fate and that we can't do anything to change the outcome. Actually, I am "on the fence," and I believe that our lives are a mixture of luck, fate, and how we handle adversity. The reason that I bring this debate up is what happened to me in the summer of 2001. I had always been a fan ever since I was in high school of the University of Virginia. I had no ties to it or affiliation with the university. I simply thought it was a great college, and I rooted for its athletic teams. After I got married, Pat and I attended all the football and basketball games. I did have some credits from attending classes at the University of Virginia Extension in Roanoke. So I was sitting at my desk at home and kind of daydreaming on that memorable day in 2001. Something made me think about UVA: Could it have been fate? Was it my destiny? And I thought to myself, *I wonder if I could get a job at UVA.*

I fired up my computer and pulled up their human resources website. To my amazement, there were 350 job openings listed. I perused the list, and it was obvious that I was not qualified for most of them. For example, elevator mechanic, brain surgeon, maintenance supervisor, etc. However, I did find a few that I had the experience, which would qualify me to be considered. To have the privilege of being a UVA employee would be a dream come true for me. I expanded my research on the internet and found the website which listed the applications that I would need to submit. I completed them and sent them in along with a résumé to the HR department. I then waited two months for a reply but never heard back from them. Several of my friends told me that it was very difficult to get hired at UVA. They also said that unless you matched their competence tests exactly, they would not even consider your application. I had no way to know if this was true or not, and I would never make that accusation. What I did know was that I would not get a job there if I sat at home and did nothing. After giving it a lot of thought, I formulated a plan and executed it immediately. I knew which department had posted the job opening, so I called and asked to speak to the manager. The person who answered told me she was not available, but if I told her why I was calling, she would transfer me to someone who could help me. When I explained the purpose of my call, she transferred me to another lady.

Our conversation went like this:

"Hello, this is Ms. Swanson [this is a fake name]. How can I help you."

"Hi, my name is Jim Cecil, and I am calling from Vinton, Virginia. I was interested in the opening you have posted."

"What are your qualifications?"

I furnished her with a quick oral sampling of my résumé.

She replied, "Oh, it sounds like you would be perfect for this position. When can you come down for an interview?"

"I can drive down whenever you can see me."

"How about in a couple of weeks, but I will have to set this up with a number of other people in the department before I can give you an exact date. I will give you a call back to let you know."

I was ecstatic that the likelihood of my becoming a UVA employee were good. A week later, I received the call from Ms. Swanson that I had been waiting for.

It was short and to the point:

"I was calling to speak to Jim Cecil."

"This is Jim, is this Ms. Swanson?"

"Yes, I wanted to get back to you concerning your job interview. I am sorry to inform you that we will not be able to offer you the job at this time. The university has placed a one year hiring freeze on all positions. We will have to evaluate our situation next year once the freeze is lifted."

I was extremely disappointed but reasoned that I still had a good job and a decent salary. One year was not a long time to wait, and I made a note on my calendar to call her back.

Exactly one year later, I was still working at Consumer Credit Counseling Service, and I did not need a reminder to call UVA back. Ms. Swanson answered the phone, and I asked her if she remembered me. She said yes and the job opening was now available. If I was interested, they would need for me to resubmit my application and résumé. We also agreed on a date for me to come in for an interview. I took the day off from work and drove to Charlottesville to meet with them. When I got there, I was escorted to a large conference room where ten men and women were waiting. They all appeared to be managers or supervisors. They asked me a lot of questions, and I was sure that I had given them satisfactory answers. When the interview was completed, one of them stated that he had two more questions which he wanted to ask me. If I was hired, I would be working with approximately forty women, and I would be the only male employee. He also stated that it seemed like I previously had been in management positions and this was not a supervisory-type of job. I told him that I had worked with women in most of my jobs and that I got along with them very well. To answer the second question, I replied that I was not looking for a management position; I simply wanted to work for the university. I left the interview feeling confident about how it had gone. They told me they wanted me to come back another day to meet several other members of the management staff before they made their final decision. The date was set, I attended the second interview, was hired on the spot, and everything fell in place after that.

UVA Experience 2003

During the next two months, Pat and I had worked hard at getting our new home set up. We also were discovering everything that Charlottesville had to offer. I was enjoying my job at UVA and trying to be involved in activities on the Grounds. We were extremely busy, and suddenly it was the Christmas holidays followed by the New Year.

We greeted 2003 full of excitement and wonderful expectations. As the year progressed, several "game-changing" events occurred. I still had not fulfilled my goal to earn a college degree. When I had started my career in banking, I had been taking classes in the evenings at the University of Virginia Extension, Roanoke College, and Virginia Western Community College in Roanoke. The banks insisted that I take bank management classes only, so I was unable to earn any other credits toward a degree. There was a community college in Charlottesville, and it seemed to make sense to me that I should enroll there to revive my pursuit of a degree. So one day on my lunch hour, I drove over to Piedmont Virginia Community College (PVCC). When I entered the building, there was a young lady seated at a table in the hallway. She motioned for me to come over to talk to her. When I walked over, she introduced herself as Kathryn Buzzoni and stated that she worked at UVA. She then asked me if I was there to sign up for some classes at PVCC, and I told her that I was trying to go back to school after forty years. We talked for a long time, and I learned that part of her job was recruiting for a program at the university called BIS, bachelor of interdisciplinary studies. The program was designed for students who could not attend day classes. BIS offered mostly classes in late-evening and nighttime sessions. After earning the required credits, you would graduate with a University of Virginia degree. She told me to get a copy of my transcripts and she would help me set up a program to begin my studies at the university.

However, things did not quite fall into place as I had hoped. To get accepted required a certain number of credits already earned. As it turned out, I lacked the number needed and had to take a few classes at PVCC after all. I signed up for classes at PVCC and also took an online class, but it would be almost a year before I could enroll at UVA. In the meantime, I was busy with my full-time job and also found a volunteer endeavor. For years the university had a "pep" band that played at football games. It was a student creation that dressed up in wild outfits and presented zany comic halftime shows. Their marching formations were reminiscent of a Chinese fire drill. Some fans liked them while the school officials considered them to be an embarrassment. The members of the band, in their efforts to be comical, sometimes went too far. The end came one year when their show, insulting the visiting team, West Virginia, was unacceptable. The university officials disbanded them and never allowed them to perform again. It was the beginning of a new era when a band director was hired and assigned the challenge of recruiting and forming a marching band to represent the university. The Cavalier Marching Band was born.

I read a newspaper article about the new band and the director, Dr. William "Bill" Pease. Dr. Pease had previously been the director of a band at a university in Michigan. He came highly recommended, and everything I read about him was positive. Also, joining Dr. Pease as an associate director was Dr. Andrew "Drew" Koch. I decided that I would call the band office and see if they were interested in having a volunteer to help them. They agreed, and I became a part of the band. Pat decided to join me, and we became a husband-and-wife volunteer team. Volunteering with the band turned out to be a ten-year experience that we have always cherished. We tried to do everything that we were asked to do while still managing to stay out of the way.

In the fall, a week before classes started, the band members were required to report for "summer camp." They were housed in a central location and spent the week getting to know each other, practicing, getting fitted for uniforms, and attending meetings. It was not "all work and no play." Programs, activities, and games were provided each night. I was always impressed with how new members were welcomed with cheers and greetings from the other students. A lot of the students were accompanied by their parents. Bill, Drew, and their assistants made sure that the family members were given a lot of attention. Bill always held a meeting for them to describe in detail the marching band program and what both the parents and their children could expect during the year. Pat and I helped by running errands, feeding meals, and anything else the students or staff needed. One of the important services we provided was to pick up students at the airport. One day when I was at work, I received a phone call from Drew.

"Jim, this is Drew, do you think you and Pat can pick up one of our students at the airport this afternoon?"

"Sure, when are they arriving?"

"It is a young lady, and her estimated time of arrival is 6:00 PM."

"That will be perfect, I will be off from work then."

"Well, there is something I need to tell you. She is coming in from Turkey, and she will be at Dulles International Airport in Washington, DC."

I agreed, and Pat and I made the trip to Dulles. Bill couldn't believe it when he was told. Once that "summer camp" had ended, the students disbursed to move into their dorms or apartments. They would be attending band practice two evenings each week. If it was a football weekend, they would practice the morning of game day. Each game had a different program, and the music and the marching formations had to be learned in a week. Game day for volunteers was an eight-hour commitment. We had to block off a road that was used to feed the band a pregame meal. Prior to the game, buses would use this same road to transport the band to the stadium. We would then have to pack up barriers that had been used to block the road and hurry over to the stadium. When we arrived at the stadium, we took our seats behind the band. It was our responsibility to watch the band members' belongings while they performed on the field. The final job for us was to feed the band their postgame meal. This meal could be some type of sandwiches or their favorite, pizza. Pat and I were volunteers for the band for ten years. We had to stop only because of my serious health issues. To Bill, Drew, every staff member, and all the students—we miss you. We will forever be grateful for the privilege of being part of the best marching band in the country—the Cavalier Marching Band.

Once more in my life I had taken on a multitude of challenges, working forty hours a week, a volunteer job, and two college courses every semester for the next five years. Of course, I also had to meet my responsibilities as a husband at home. What I did not know was that my life was about to be compounded by an onslaught of health issues.

2004

In the fall of 2004, I attended my first BIS class, nationalism. My professor was Ann Marie Plunkett, who in my final year was assigned to me as my mentor. It was exciting for me to be back in the classroom, especially with much younger students. I found it to be invigorating and rejuvenating. I got along exceptionally well with Ann Marie and later had her for some other courses. Attending two three-hour classes each week was a challenge, but the most time-consuming aspect was the homework assignments. Normally you would be required to complete a reading assignment or research a topic. There were also reports or creative papers to write. Fortunately, Pat understood that we would not be seeing each other much due to my commitment to my studies. I signed up for summer classes as well as the fall and spring sessions. When they were available, I would take classes named J-term. These classes were taught during the break beginning on January 2 and running until regular classes resumed in February. You could take only one class at a time, and you were required to attend three sessions a week. It was designed as a "blitz" program to pick up three credit hours in only a few weeks. I also signed up for a few "online" classes, which enabled me to work from home by using my computer.

2005

Everything—my job, the band volunteering, and classes—was going well for me. I was staying busy, working hard, and enjoying the university experience. I had often heard that when your health fails, other things in your life tend to shrink to insignificance. Unfortunately, I was about to find out. I had issues with high blood pressure and sleep apnea. As I have already documented, I spent most of my life "burning the candle at both ends," working two jobs, being active in volunteer endeavors, and going to school. It had to be the fact that I had been younger then, but I had no intentions of slowing down.

My body had other ideas and proved to me that it was going to override my plans. In October of 2005, I suffered a heart attack. I underwent a heart catherization, which revealed several blocked arteries. Stints were implanted to provide better blood flow. Of course, I was stubborn and missed only a few days of work and no classroom time.

2006

In 2006 I was coasting along, enjoying my newfound life in Charlottesville. When I went into work each morning, I thought about how fortunate I was to be working at the University of Virginia. My classes were going well, and I had completed twelve courses. I had worked hard and earned an A in every subject. Signing up for the BIS program had been a godsend, and I owed it all to Kathryn Buzzoni. She, along with everyone in the BIS office, had become my good friends who were always encouraging me to excel. I had a wonderful wife, a great daughter, and a super grandson. Simply put, my life was perfect. Unfortunately, the blue skies and sunshine were about to give way to dark clouds, terrible thunder, and lightning. It was extremely serious and proved to be the supreme test of my fortitude and will.

It was a cold fall Saturday in September, which, for some reason, reminded me of the day my father had left forty-nine years ago. It was also a Saturday football game day. Pat and I had helped the band and had put in a full day. We arrived at the house, and I was in the bathroom standing in front of the vanity. Suddenly my legs folded under me, and I collapsed to the floor. I lay in a heap on the floor and could not move my legs. Pat called the rescue squad, and they transported me to the emergency room. After undergoing a multitude of x-rays, MRIs, and other tests, it was determined that I was totally paralyzed from the waist down. They admitted me to the hospital, but did not discuss my problem any further. Several days later, a small group of doctors and interns came to the room to talk to Pat and me. The spokesperson in the group was a spinal surgeon named Francis H. Shen. He explained to us that I had suffered a degeneration of the cervical interververtebral disc—or, simpler said, degenerative arthritis of the spine. He confirmed that I was paralyzed from the waist down and explained what my options were. If I agreed to have a nine-hour spinal operation, there was a 50 percent chance that I would walk again (which also meant that there would be a 50 percent chance I would never walk again). If I chose to not have surgery, it would be certain that I would remain paralyzed and would have to spend the remainder of my life in a wheelchair. As they like to say, "It was a no-brainer," so I opted to put my life in his hands.

The surgery was performed, and afterward the doctors considered it to be a success. Dr. Shen told me that I now had fifty-eight staples and two steel rods in my back. He also confessed to me six months later that he had taken one of my ribs out and had used it to repair my spine. However, there was one huge problem. They also said that I was still paralyzed and I would have months of intensive physical therapy in a rehabilitation center to learn how to walk. Several weeks later, I was transferred to my new home at the rehab center. I spent six months at Health South, the University of Virginia

Rehabilitation Center. When I first got there, I had no feeling or strength in my lower body. The only way I could get out of bed was with the help of two therapists who would lift my legs up and place them on a wooden board so that I could slide down into a wheelchair. When I was discharged from there, I had to report twice a week for several months for more therapy at the Health South Outpatient Clinic. Following that I had a nurse and a therapist come to my house twice a week for in-home therapy sessions. The results of these many months of physical therapy were a complete recovery. I started in a wheelchair and then graduated next to a walker. After that I used a cane and then a walking stick until I finally was able to walk like a normal person.

When people found out about my condition and recovery, they would say to me, "I don't know how you did it." My answer was, "It is like this, no matter what happens in life, you either keep going or you just give up. I will never give up." The way that I have persevered in life is to always keep a good attitude, never lose your sense of humor, and never feel sorry for yourself. Also always, in any situation, be humble and grateful for what you have been blessed with.

During this period of time, I was on short-term disability from my job. The BIS staff understood my situation and were thoughtful and considerate. They allowed me to complete the two classes that had been interrupted by my hospitalization. My two professors, Dr. William Welty and Lawrence Wieder, agreed to meet me one-on-one to complete the required courses.

2007–2008

When the spring classes were posted, I signed up for two despite being in my wheelchair. No one seemed to mind, and I was thankful that I did not attract attention. I continued to make progress on my quest for complete recovery. In June I returned to work full-time, and I also signed up for two summer classes. So it was full steam ahead, and the "Jim Cecil train" was back in business. But just as "the train" was regaining momentum, there was a derailment and a crash.

I suffered my second heart attack. Despite having yet another health setback, I was determined to beat the odds and to not let this discourage me. When my friends asked me about it, I explained to them that I was treating it as "just another bump in the road." I missed no classroom time for my summer sessions and enrolled for two more subjects for the fall term.

In January, I enrolled in a J-term class to pick up three more credit hours in a one-month session. I followed that with two more classes for the spring term. I was getting close to completing my journey to become a University of Virginia graduate. While I was sure that I would accomplish this long-sought-after goal, I probably was also overconfident. I was suddenly knocked off my self-made pedestal and brought back down to earth when my old nemesis struck again. I suffered my third heart attack. This time I had the heart attack and was taken to the emergency room on a Saturday. I was then discharged the next day on Sunday. On Monday, I was back in the classroom. It did not seem important to me to let the professor or the students know. Somehow, he found out, and he asked me the following week if it was true. When I confirmed it, he shook his head in disbelief. He said, "You know, you are amazing."

THE CAPSTONE PROJECT

FALL 2008 TO SPRING 2009

After finishing my two spring classes, it was time to enroll in two more for the summer. Once those two classes were finished, I was really close to completing the last required credits I needed to graduate. The last two semesters, fall term 2008 and spring term 2009, were different from the rest of the classes that I had taken. In order for BIS students to be awarded their degrees, they had to complete a Capstone Project.

The website for the School of Continuing and Professional Studies, Degree, Bachelor of Interdisciplinary Studies defines the Capstone Project as follows:

> The Capstone Project is a two semester process in which students pursue independent research on a question or problem of their choice, engage with the scholarly debates in the relevant disciplines, and—with the guidance of a faculty mentor—produce a substantial paper that reflects a deep understanding of the topic.
>
> Students are strongly encouraged to choose a topic in which they have some competence based on their academic work, professional experience, or future career options. The Capstone Project is both a valuable intellectual experience and also a vehicle through which students can demonstrate their research, analytical and writ-

ing skills to either prospective employers or graduate and professional schools.

In addition to these stipulations, the Capstone website states the following:

> Capstone Framework & Guidelines—A Capstone Project must demonstrate the following characteristics. Each characteristic can be satisfied in deferent ways depending on the topic, discipline and the approach taken. But, taken together, they represent the capstone framework Originally—You must reach your own deep understanding of a clearly designed and focused topic. You must formulate your own perspective on an issue and draw your own conclusions. The final project and form of presentation can also draw upon your originality and creativity.

> Independence—Although you will have a capstone mentor as a guide and domain expert, you will work primarily on your own.

> Appropriate Scope—The Cap Stone Project is equivalent to a six credit course. Therefore you should plan to spend at least as much time on your Capstone Project within a limited scope.

> Orderly & Objective Process Of Inquiry—The Capstone Project demonstrates your facility with the methods of inquiry. These include your ability to ask the right questions, to synthesize ideas, to draw and support conclusions, to recognize compelling research, to communicate your ideas, or to solve a problem using a specific set of tools.

> Presentation—Students will make a presentation
> to an audience of students, family members and
> faculty.

My first priority was to find a mentor from the BIS faculty. I asked Anne Marie Plunkett if she would be willing to serve in that capacity. I had her for several of my classes, and we had always had a good rapport. She agreed, and we were both pleased. The next challenge was to decide on a topic. I had always been interested in military history, especially the civil war. I had a number of books about this in my library at home. A lot of battles were fought on Virginia soil, and there still remains numerous battlefields. Also, many of the Confederate officers were Virginia natives. In addition to this, I had taken an on line course about the civil war (not a BIS course). So I selected my Capstone Project to be "the civil war." What a mistake that turned out to be. I was checking out ten to twelve books a week at the Alderman Library. I was drowning in research and getting nowhere. Fortunately, I realized that I must minimize my topic in order to concentrate on one issue or aspect pertaining to the civil war. I was meeting with Anne Marie every couple of weeks, and she recognized this problem immediately. I tried several topics "on for size," and each time she said I needed to make it more defined.

As a result, the title of my Capstone Project was "Slavery as a Profitable Labor System in the Antebellum South." I knew slavery was a controversial subject, and I had a multitude of issues to pick from, such as, religious, moral, social, and economics. My Capstone Project concentrated on economic factors only. That did not mean that other issues were not important nor that I approved of slavery. During the Antebellum period, 1800–1860, plantations grew in size, and the demand for slave labor became greater and greater. My theory was that slavery was a highly profitable labor system which brought great wealth to plantation owners. It was instrumental in the economic development of the South. To prove my theory, I calculated the production level of a slave compared to a free hired laborer. I then deducted expenses and cost from the gross profit to determine the net profit. The results were conclusive that the slave outproduced the freeman and created a much higher net profit for his owner. It also was capable of producing enormous amounts of wealth. On the eve of the civil war, the slave South had achieved a level of per capital wealth not matched by other countries until the eve of World War II.

My Capstone Project enabled me to utilize and further develop analytical, research, and writing skills previously learned during my years in the bachelor of interdisciplinary studies.

GRADUATION

I had reached the end of my formal BIS education. My Capstone Project had ended with my oral presentation before various members of the BIS faculty, other professors, students, friends, family members, and other relatives. I was satisfied with my oratorical skills and my performance before a large crowd. With that out of the way, I was looking forward to all the excitement and happiness that go with graduation day. At the University of Virginia, there is an area that is called the Lawn. It is part of the original university designed and built by Thomas Jefferson in 1826. He named it his Academical Village, and it extends from the Rotunda at the north end to Cabell Hall at the south. It is framed on either side by the pavilions, which house distinguished faculty members and living quarters for student leaders. A rocky ridge running north to south necessitated lying the lawn out in four two-hundred-foot-wide terraces with the rotunda sitting at the ridges peak. The Lawn is 355 feet in length and the graduates "walk the Lawn" after forming on the rotunda.

On graduation day, I was still unable to walk long distances and climb stairs. I asked permission to sit at the bottom of the rotunda steps so that I could join my BIS students as they passed by. There was no way that I was going to miss "walking the Lawn." Because I had graduated with honors, I was wearing a colored stole over my gown. Several times people stopped to ask me for directions, addressing me as "Professor." I guess it was not only the stole, but my age and my grayish hair.

This also happened one day when I had tried to purchase a book from the bookstore for one of my classes. They were out of the book, and I asked one of the clerks when they would get them in. His reply was, "We have your books for your class on order, Doctor."

Graduation day was a wonderful event for me. Having started my quest for a degree forty-nine years ago made it all the more gratifying and special. My only regret was that my mother and Bill were no longer around to see how I had turned out.

CELEBRITY

Prior to graduation day, I suddenly was made aware that I had obtained some sort of notoriety. In writing this story of my life, I have tried to simply explain how I was able to overcome adversity and defy the odds. I have never thought of myself as anything special. When I applied for jobs, I was always uncomfortable "tooting my own horn" on résumés. It has always been difficult for me to accept and react to praise. While I appreciate the compliments, I don't handle flattery very well.

One day, several weeks before graduation, I was sitting in my cubicle when a young man and a lady introduced themselves. They stated that they were from CBS Channel 19 News to do an interview with me. They asked for my permission, and when I agreed, they began filming. They had been advised that I was the oldest graduate at age sixty-seven and also told of the health trials and tribulations I had to overcome. The next day the station's news anchor, Bo Sykes, carried the interview. He added a comment, "Cecil's GPA (grade point average) was 3.80 out of a possible 4.00 while working full-time, that is impressive." Little did I know that this was just the beginning of a long list of interviews, newspaper articles, internet postings, and congratulatory e-mails. I was overwhelmed with all the attention. It was a feature on National TV on ABC and on Google. I received e-mails from strangers in other states who stated how inspired they were when they heard my story. One teacher from Texas sent me an e-mail in which she explained how she read my story to her class.

I have never understood what was so special, but I can honestly say that I owe it all to my many well-wishers, friends, relatives, and those who wrote to me and about me.

I would also be remiss if I did not include my professors, my doctors, my coworkers, the BIS staff, and my family members (especially my wife, Pat, and my daughter, Anne). No matter how much adversity I faced in life, I was never alone. In all my accomplishments, all my challenges, all my battles, and all my victories, I was just a small component. My life story has been forged by others, and I was just along for the ride.

I have explained my few moments of glory. So the following pages contain a collage of sorts giving you a mix of samples of news clippings, interviews, e-mails, hoopla, and sensational hype.

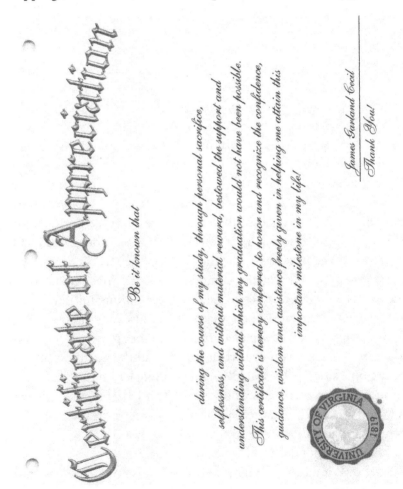

Certificate of Appreciation

Be it known that

during the course of my study, through personal sacrifice, selflessness, and without material reward, bestowed the support and understanding without which my graduation would not have been possible. This certificate is hereby conferred to honor and recognize the confidence, guidance, wisdom and assistance freely given in helping me attain this important milestone in my life!

James Garland Cecil

Thank You!

UNIVERSITY OF VIRGINIA 1819

Cecil, James (jgc4d)
From: Plasket, Donna
Sent: Monday, March 02,200910:14 AM
To: Donna Plasket
Subject: Beta Iota Sigma chapter of Alpha Sigma Lambda

To our BIS high achievers,

I am delighted to tell' you that your academic record at the University of Virginia has qualified you for membership in the Beta Iot a Sigma chapter of Alpha Sigma Lambda, considered the premier national honor society for students in adult baccalaureate degree programs. Congratulations.

Alpha Sigma Lambda is a nonprofit organization devoted to the advancement of scholarship and to the recognition of nontraditional students continuing their higher education. The Society was established in 1945-46 to honor superior scholarship and leadership in adult students who are accomplishing academic excellence while facing competing responsibilities of family, community, and work.

You clearly have earned this honor, and I look forward to your accepting membership in the Society.

Our induction ceremony for new members will take place on Thursday evening. May 7,6:00, at Pavilion I on West Lawn, site of your orientation reception. Current faculty members of Beta Iot a Sigma will be present and will officiate at the ceremony. While we have designed it to be a meaningful experience for you, the ceremony itself will be short and fairly informal; and you will not be required to prepare anything, just to repeat tire honor society pledge led by a faculty member. A reception will follow, and you are welcome to bring family members or other guests. If any of you from Tidewater will not able to attend, you still will be able to become members and receive your recognition materials.

The national organization does not require individual member dues. BIS pays for our chapter membership. The original members of our chapter determined that a $25 annual fee to be paid by each member in the spring is appropriate to sustain the organization and to make special events and recognitions possible. President David Barrett will contact you regarding dues.

It is a major mark of achievement for BIS that we were approved for a chapter of Alpha Sigma Lambda, and particularly that each year we have a large number of students who exceed the minimum standards established by the national organization. Once you accept membership in our chapter, you have life membership in Alpha Sigma Lambda.

Again, congratulations. We are very proud of your accomplishments.

Please let me know if you accept membership and if you will be available to participate in the induction ceremony on May 7.

Thank you, and all the best for a productive and fulfilling second half of spring term.

Regards,
Donna
Donna Plasket Director
Bachelor of Interdisciplinary Studies
University of Virginia
106 Midmont Lane

P.O. Box 400764
Charlottesville, Virginia 22904-4764 434
243.2557 (phone)

GOALS OF ALPHA SIGMA LAMBDA

The Alpha Sigma Lambda National Honor Society was established in 1946 to honor superior scholarship and leadership in adult students. It is not only the oldest, but also the largest chapter-based honor society for full- and part-time adult students. Today, with chapters at over 250 colleges and universities throughout the United States, Alpha Sigma Lambda provides a truly prestigious opportunity to recognize the special achievements of adult students who accomplish academic excellence while facing competing interests of family, work, and community.

For the nontraditional students, the society stands as an inspiration for continued scholastic growth, a builder of pride through recognition, and an invitation to associate with similarly motivated students. For the chapter institution, the society serves as a vehicle for imparting appreciation for adult students' academic achievements and contributions.

NEW MEMBERS

Students

John T. Ashley, Jr.
Nicholas Bartley
Matthew J. Bowyer
William John Brase
Amber Rene Brister

James G. Cecil
Joseph K. Dunham
Lynn E. Harris
Jane Beblich
Michelle C. Mattocks
Michael W. Moses
Eric B. Newsome
Charlene L. Pattison
John Ryan
Wynter C. Shotten
BB Slaven
Sandra Lee Smith
Michelle E. Stump
Sara B. Teaster
Jody M. Weedlun
Ellynne L. Woodson

FACULTY

Billy K. Cannaday, Dean, SCPS, University of Virginia
Clifford W. Haury, Dean, Humanities, Fine Arts and Sciences, PVCC

Sigma Alpha Lambda Press Release

Sigma Alpha Lambda is proud to announce that James G. Cecil of Palmyra, VA, has recently become recognized as a member of Sigma Alpha Lambda, National Leadership and Honors Organization at the University of Virginia. Sigma Alpha Lambda is a national leadership and honors organization dedicated to promoting and rewarding academic achievement and providing members with opportunities for community service, personal development, and lifelong professional fulfillment. Congratulations to James G. Cecil.

May 14, 2009

Rain or shine, one University of Virginia student is ready for his chance to walk across the lawn. It's a day that's been 67 years in the making.

Jim Cecil is 67 years old; He'll probably stand out a little this weekend among the crowd of twenty-something graduates. He says his life experience has made him value his new degree and the journey to get it more than if he'd followed a traditional path.

"I looked at it and I thought gee this would really be a lot of fun just to be a student again. I haven't regretted it and it is one of the best things I have ever done in my life," says Cecil.

Cecil plugged away for six years going to night school to earn his Bachelor of Interdisciplinary Studies. He says he decided to go to college because he felt it was a part of life he'd missed out on.

JIM CECIL

130

UVATODAY
TOP NEWS FROM THE UNIVERSITY OF VIRGINIA

U.Va. News
News Releases
News by Category
U.Va. Profiles
Faculty Opinion
News Videos
U.Va. Blogs
UVA Today Radio

Headlines @ U.Va.

Inside U.Va.
Announcements
For Faculty/Staff
Accolades
Off the Shelf
In Memoriam

UVA Today Blog

For Journalists

All Publications

About Us

Subscribe To
Daily Report E-News
RSS News Feeds
Podcasts/Vodcasts

Search U.Va. News

Keyword / Name

2006–09 News
Go

After 50 Years, U.Va. Dreams Fulfilled For Oldest Grad Jim Cecil

May 19, 2009 – Ever since he graduated from high school in 1960, Jim Cecil dreamed of working for or graduating from the University of Virginia — even though all of his family are Virginia Tech fans.

After living in the Roanoke area for the first 60 years of his life, he moved to Charlottesville in 2002 to start living his dream of working at U.Va. On Sunday, after six years of evening classes, he fulfilled the second part of his dream, receiving a Bachelor of Independent Studies degree from the School of Continuing and Professional Studies.

For years, Cecil, 67, told friends and coworkers that he'd walk the Lawn and retire on the same day. But the oldest undergraduate in U.Va.'s Class of 2009 won't be retiring for at least a few more years, because he's still having too much fun living his dream.

"I love being here and being part of the University," Cecil said. "I'd almost work for nothing, because I love my job, I love U.Va., I love the people I work with."

While working at U.Va. as an accounts receivable specialist has been a dream come true for Cecil, heading back into the classroom to finish his undergraduate degree more than 30 years after he had last taken college classes (at the U.Va. Extension Center in Roanoke and two other Roanoke-area colleges) may be the best thing he's ever done, Cecil said — adding with a smile that he hopes his wife of 25 years doesn't read that.

Besides getting a kick out of occasionally being mistaken for a professor, taking classes with fellow students mostly in their 20s and 30s has been rejuvenating, he said. "I've probably never really grown up," he explained.

Although the soft-spoken Cecil focuses on how he has benefited from his classmates, the benefits have been mutual, according to his teachers.

"A true gentleman, Jim Cecil contributes to the learning of his classmates with generosity and candor," said Charlotte Matthews, a writing instructor in the SCPS. "Effulgence emanates from him as he strives to gain all he can from the subjects before him."

Cecil's professors also admire how he has persevered through several serious health crises. In the spring of 2007, he suddenly collapsed at home and was paralyzed from the waist down, due to degenerative spinal problems. After a nine-hour operation in which bone from his shin was used to reinforce his spine, Cecil spent nine months in intensive physical therapy relearning how to walk.

He missed a few classes, but still earned his credits that semester. "I'm not one of these people who want to sit on the front porch in a rocker," he said. "You either give up, or you do what you need to do to get back."

Even two heart attacks did little to slow Cecil down. After the second, he was back in class the next day and didn't bother to tell his teachers until weeks later.

"Jim has faced some serious health issues that would have daunted most of us, but he carried on with determination and an optimistic and uncomplaining spirit," said Ann Marie Plunkett, a SCPS faculty member in social sciences.

On top of working full time and overcoming health challenges on his six-year journey to his degree, Cecil earned a 3.8 grade point average and induction into the Alpha Sigma Lambda National Honor Society.

For Cecil, U.Va. represents a standard of excellence. "A gentleman once told me, 'Everything you do in life, do it with quality,' and I think that's what the University of Virginia does."

— By Brevy Cannon

Jim Cecil

(Photo: Dan Addison)

- Print this story
- Email this story

Contact:
H. Brevy Cannon
General Assignments Writer
(434) 243-0368
brevy@virginia.edu

John T. Casteen III, President of the University of Virginia Graduation Speech, May 17, 2009

Some 6,280 graduates and their families and guests—35,000 persons in all—gathered on the weekend of May 16–17 for Finals 2009. The following is a small excerpt from President Casteen's address.

Dear Alumni, Parents, and Friends in the University Community The University's founder, Thomas Jefferson, promoted what he called "an aristocracy of virtue and talent." He intended this to be an aristocracy based, not on privilege, but on personal accomplishment.

In the lives of our students in this Class of 2009, we see stories of great fortitude, determination, and perseverance in the face of tragedy.

An example is Jim Cecil who will receive his Bachelor of Independent Study degree today from the School of Continuing and Professional Studies. Jim works full time at the University as an account's receivable specialist, and has been taking evening classes for six years. Two years ago, he was paralyzed from the waist down, owing to degenerative spinal problems. He went through a nine-hour operation and nine months of physical therapy to learn to walk again. At 67, Jim is the oldest person completing an undergraduate degree at the University this year.

Jim also received the following congratulations:

Congratulations on your achievement today. May you have continued success in the years ahead.

Sincerely,
The Seven Society

Cecil, James (jgc4d)
From: Cannon, Henry (hbc2t)
Sent: Wednesday, May 20, 2009 4:23 PM
To: Meg Hibbert
CC: jgc4d@virginia.edu; Dan Addison Re: Excellent story on Jim Cecil

Meg,

Thanks for your interest in Jim and your kind words about my story.

You're welcome to use Dan Addison's photo. You can download a high res version from:

http://www.Virginia.edu/uvatodav/news-Release.php?id=8747#

Please credit: Dan Addison / U.Va. Public Affairs

No charge for the reprint.

Jim is copied on this email and his contact info is: Jim Cecil

jgc4d (Svirginia. edu Office Phone: 924-4046

I look forward to reading the Salem Times-Register article. Will it be available on your website? If so, we'll link to it from U.Va. Today.

best,
Brevy

P.S. Jim's story also attracted coverage by our local TV station, WCAV:

http://www.charlottesvillenewsplex.tv/news/headlines/45017557.html

And that story was picked up nationally by ABC News, so Jim's been getting congratulation calls from old friends in NC and elsewhere. I'm sure he'll appreciate hearing from his Salem friends, thanks to your article.

On 5/20/09 3:40 PM, Meg Hibbert <meg(
amainstreetnewspapers.com> wrote:

Dear Brevy:

That is an excellent story you wrote on
Salem, Va., native Jim Cecil. One of his classmates sent it to us. Our Salem Times-Register
plans to write a short feature about him, and
would like to reprint the accompanying photograph taken by Dan Addison. Would you please
pass along this request to Dan or tell me whom I
should contact about reprint permission. We will
give photo credit.

Also, do you have a phone number or e-mail
for Jim Cecil for me to double-check some Salem
information with him?

Thank you for your help.

From: Cecil, James (jgc4d)
Sent: Monday, May 18,200911:24 AM
To: Nimax, Gary (gsn6x)
Subject: RE: 67-Year-Old Student to Graduate from the University of Virginia

Gary,

Thanks for the e-mail and the offer of a photograph. I think I saw you in the crowd yesterday-were you standing to our left as we walked down the Lawn? It was an extremely exciting and tiring day for me. I am a calm "laid back" kind of guy and all the attention has been a bit overwhelming. At the same time, I appreciate everyone's kindness.

And yes, I would love to have a copy of the photo.

Thanks again,
Jim

Jim Cecil
Accounts Receivable Specialist
Revenue and Collections
FINANCIAL ADMINISTRATION
UNIVERSITY OF VIRGINIA
Carruthers Hall
P.0. Box 400201
(Charlottesville, VA 22903
ph: 434-924-4046/ fax: 434-924-1034
email address jgc4d(a)virginia.edu

Confidentiality Statement: This email message, including any attachments, is for sole use of the intended recipient and may contain confidential and privileged information. Any unauthorized review, use, disclosure, or distribution is prohibited.

If you are not the intended recipient, please contact the sender by reply email and delete the original and all copies of this email.

Original Message
From: Nimax, Gary (gsn6x)
Sent: Monday, May 18, 2009 9:50 AM To: Cecil, James (jgc4d)
Subject: FW: 67-Year-Old Student to Graduate from the University of Virginia

Jim—congratulations! I'm so proud of you for getting your degree. I'm sure it was difficult to continue at times, while working full-time and dealing with such serious medical issues. You are a good reminder that it is never too late to go after your dreams.

A friend of mine since childhood, Ron Phillips, was walking down the Lawn right next to you. We took the photo of Ron, but then I noticed you were in it too. I'll have to share a copy with you.

Best wishes
Gary
Original Message

From: Cecil, James (jgc4d)
Sent: Monday, May 18, 2009 8:20 AM
To: 'Evelyn Edson'
Subject: RE: Walking the lawn

Dear Evelyn,

Thank you so much for thinking of me. Yesterday was a very special day and the culmination of six years of hard work. I owe it all to the BIS staff and all my wonderful professors like you. Every time I see a map now I think of you. Again, thanks for remembering me and perhaps our paths will cross again in the future-l certainly hope so.

Jim

Jim Cecil
Accounts Receivable Specialist
Revenue and Collections
FINANCIAL ADMINISTRATION
UNIVERSITY OF VIRGINIA
Carruthers Hall
P.O. Box 400201
Charlottesville, VA 22903
ph: 434-924-4046/ fax: 434-924-1034
email address iqc4d@virqinia.edu

From: Evelyn Edson
Sent: Sunday, May 17, 2009 1:27
PM To: jgc4d@virginia.edu
Subject: Walking the lawn

Dear Jim: Thinking of you today, "walking the Lawn," as you said you'd do. Congratulations on your achievement. With all best wishes,

Evelyn Edson
Professor Emerita of History
Piedmont Virginia Community College
Address: 268 Springtree Lane
Scottsville, VA 24590
(434) 286-3466

New book: Ingrid Baumgartner and Hartmut Kugler, eds., Europa im Weltbild des Mittelalters (Berlin: Akademie Verlag, 2008). My chapter is "Dacia ubi et Gothia: Die nordostliche Grenze Europas in der mittelalterlichen Kartographie." Off prints (or English version) available upon request.

CONFIDENTIALITY NOTICE: This e-mail message, including any attachments, is for the sole use of the intended recipient(s) and may contain confidential and privileged information or otherwise be protected by law. Any access, use, disclosure or distribution of this email message by anyone other than the intended.

From: Cannon Henry (hbc2t)
Sent: Wednesday, May 13,200912:44 PM
To: skip.forbes@wcav.tv
Cc: Dillard, Carolyn (cem9v); Rebecca Arrington; jgc4d@viiginia.edu
Subject: Jim Cecil summary for WCAV

Skip,

Here's the info on Jim Cecil. He will make a great interview and graduate story. By copying him on this, I'm giving him a heads up that you'll be in touch today for an interview.

Jim Cecil, age 67, is the oldest person completing an undergraduate degree at the University this year. He is graduating with a Bachelor of Interdisciplinary Studies (BIS) degree from U.Va.'s School of Continuing and Professional Studies, and this happens to be the 10th year of the BIS program.

he is described by the SCPS as "just one of those all-round good guys who would win the model student/citizen award if there were such a thing." He works full-time at the University as an Accounts Receivable Specialist, and has been taking evening classes for 6 years now, doing 2 classes a semester. He is also a volunteer assistant to the U.Va. Marching Band.

During his 6 years of studies, he has persevered through a couple of pretty serious health crises. 2.5 years ago he collapsed at home and was paralyzed from waist down, due to degenerative spinal problems. He went through a 9 hour operation and 9 months of intensive physical therapy to totally re-learn how to walk again.

"I'm not one of these people who want to sit on the front porch in a rocker," he says. "You either give up, or you do what you need to do to get back."

He also has had 2 heart attacks, 1 of which, the day later he was back in class.

He's been married for 35 years, and has one grown daughter and one grandson, age 2.

He's originally from the Roanoke area and had lived in that area all his life until he moved to Charlottesville in 2602 to work for the University of Virginia, which had been a lifelong dream. Even though all of his family and his wife's family are Virginia Tech fans, he's always been a U.Va. fan from back when he graduated high school. For many years before moving here he would travel over from Roanoke to watch U.Va. football games.

Contact info:
Jim Cecil jgc4d@virginia.edu
Office Phone: 924-4046
H. Brevy Cannon
General Assignment Writer
University of Virginia Media Relations
(434) 243-0368
Fax-(434) 924-0938
brevvOvirginia.edu
UVA Today: http://www.Virginia.edu/uvatodav/

From: Becky Marshall [musicmarshalls@yahoo. com]
Sent: Tuesday, May 26,20091:35 PM
To: Cecil, James G'gc4d)
Cc: Matt Marshall
Subject: RE: Thank you so much!

No need to send a formal thank you. Your email is thanks enough. I thought you might be proud to own a special BIS UVA sweat shirt (even though I'm sure it is too large for you) but it will keep you warm at the winter football games.

So glad you'd like to spend more time with us. We love everything you mentioned; cards, games, movies, and always food. Our apartment complex also has a lovely pool with outdoor jacuzzi so dinner and swim would great at our place too. Let us know when is a good time to get together.

On Tue, 5/26/09, Cecil, James (jgc4d) <jgc4d@
sservices.virginia,edu> wrote:
From: Cecil, James (jgc4d)
Subject: RE: Thank you so much!
To: "Becky Marshall" <musicmarshalls@yahoo.
com>
Date: Tuesday, May 26,2009,3:48 PM

Becky,

We were so glad that you and Matt came
Saturday. It was such a special day for me and for
my whole family. I tried to get around and talk to
everyone and my only regret is that I did not have
more time to spend with them. I will be sending
you a formal thank you for the sweat shirt and I
will tell you now that I appreciate it.

Yes, we would like to do something with
you guys-what do you like to do-play cards, go to
movies, concerts, eat out?

We will be in touch,

Jim

Jim Cecil
Accounts Receivable Specialist
Revenue and Collections
FINANCIAL ADMINISTRATION
UNIVERSITY OF VIRGINIA
Carruthers Hall
P.O. Box 400201

From: Griggs, Terrie (tag5v)
Sent: Wednesday, May 20, 200910:09 AM
To: Cecil, James (jgc4d)
Subject: Graduation

Dear Mr. Cecil,

I read in UVA Today, about your graduation from UVA's SCPS program and I just wanted to say congratulations and that your story inspired me. As a person who also went back to school as an adult (University of West Florida 2003) I know how hard it is to go back and persevere. I was in my 30's and had the support of my family (husband and 2 kids) and the Veteran's Administration, but it was still tough. I like to think that I inspired my children academically, I hope so anyway.

I am also a huge fan of UVa, of the people, and of my amazing job in which people like you and the things that we as a University do for not just the students but the world (in terms of research, education, and inspiration) brighten each and every day. We are immensely lucky in our professions and this university.

I can't begin to understand what you went through with your health problems, but you remind all of us that it's never too late to look at life from fresh eyes and to keep trucking. So Mr. Cecil, thank you for your story and from one late-in-life graduate to another I salute you and thank you for inspiring me today.

Keep growing younger but brighter.

Sincerely,
Terrie A. Griggs, USAF Veteran
IT Associate
Development & Public Affairs
400 Ray C. Hunt Dr.
Charlottesville, VA 22904

From: Richard or Donna Browder
Sent: Monday, May 18, 2009 12:11 AM
To: Jim Cecil
Subject: Graduation Photos
Attachments: Cecil, Jim's Graduation May 17, 2009 002.JPG; Cecil, Jim's Graduation May 17, 2009 003. JPG; Cecil, Jim's Graduation May 17, 2009 004. JPG; Cecil, Jim's Graduation May 17, 2009 005.JPG; Cecil, Jim's Graduation May 17, 2009 006.JPG; Cecil, Jim's Graduation May 17, 2009 010.JPG

Jim,

I had a great time today....thank you for letting me be a part of your special day. It was nice meeting your wonderful family.

Special thanks again to Pat for the delicious lunch.

More pictures to follow... J split them up to keep files smaller.

See you Saturday,
Richard

From: Becky Marshall

Jim and Pat,

Matt and I want to thank you so much for including us in your delightful graduation cele-bration on Sat. We had the most wonderful time and it was so moving to see you, your family, and many lifelong friends expressing such joy. The lunch was marvelous, the company even better. Your examination was fun and the final singing of the Good Ole Song was most appropriate.

Matt and I count ourselves lucky to call you Mends and would love to meet for lunch for or dinner when convenient Keep in touch.

Becky

From: Plasket, Donna (dp4q)
Sent: Sunday, May 24, 2009 7:03 AM
To: Cecil, James Qgc4d)
Subject: Thank you

Jim and Pat, what a lovely luncheon. Thank you so much for including us.

You have much of which to be proud, and we were honored to be among those celebrating with you.

All the best to you and your family, and we'll see you again soon, I'm sure.

Regards,
Donna

From: Meg Hibbert
Sent: Friday, June 05, 2009 12:57 PM
To: Cecil, James (jgc4d)
Subject: Re: Newspaper Article
JimCeci...rtf

Dear Jim,

The article was on the front page of the Salem Times-Register on June 4, with a cutout of you reading one of your congratulations cards. I'm sure you're going to get comments from your friends about how proud they are of you.

Our website is unavailable right now, so I'm sending you the text of the article until OurValley.org is rebuilt, and also pasting it below.

I'm putting it in the folder for a future issue of The Vinton Messenger, too, so if there are any glaring errors that need correcting, please let me know before Tuesday.

Thanks for your help in capturing the real Jim Cecil. I hope I did.

Meg

CECIL GRADUATES FROM COLLEGE 49 YEARS LATER

By Meg Hibbert

When Jim Cecil graduated from Andrew Lewis High School in 1960, he dreamed of someday getting a college degree from the University of Virginia.

Forty-nine years later, he did. On May 17 the 67-year-old took the traditional walk on The Lawn at the college founded by Thomas Jefferson, and accepted his Bachelor of Interdisciplinary Studies degree from the School of Continuing and Professional Studies. The oldest member of the class of 2009 earned a grade point average of 3.8 while working frill time and volunteering with the University of Virginia's Cavalier Marching Band.

He also met the challenge of health problems, including two heart attacks and an operation to that involved removing one of his ribs and using it to repair his degenerating spine, which is anchored by two large metal screws.

"It was kind of fun being in class with younger people," said Cecil in a telephone interview from his home near Charlottesville, at Lake Monticello in Fluvanna County. "It kick-started me. At that age and 35 years of marriage, it was nice to have a challenge and work toward something." Because he has silver hair, sometimes he was mistaken for a professor, said Cecil, who had started his undergraduate degree taking college classes at the University of Virginia Extension Center in Roanoke and two other Roanoke-area colleges.

He earned his degree through six years of night classes in the program designed for working people. He works in the revenue collections department and is an accounts receivable specialist. And no, he has no plans to retire soon, although he originally kidded that he would "walk The Lawn and retire the same day."

"I'm just having too much fun," Cecil said, laughing.

When he and Pat lived in the Roanoke Valley, Cecil followed UVA's athletic teams and made contributions to the athletic fund, he said. He had an 18-year-career in banking and worked for First /Virginia, First Union, Dominion and National Bank of Blacksburg, he said.

Seven years ago he accepted the position at UVA, so they sold their house and moved.

"We still have a lot of friends in Salem and Roanoke," he said. "My love for UVA is second only to my love of Andrew Lewis and Salem." He still has his monogram letter from when he played defense on the ALHS football team, as a nose guard and defensive tackle. He was also on the track team.

His friends in Salem are mighty proud of Cecil.

"Those of us who knew him in high school are so proud of him, of anybody who has the perseverance," said Brenda Lipscomb, formerly

Deyerley, who was three years behind him at Andrew Lewis.

Cecil and his wife, who is from Martinsville, met while she was teaching in Roanoke County, at William Byrd. Eventually they moved over to Vinton while she was teaching math, and their daughter, now Anne Cecil Booker, was in the band at William Byrd. She and her husband, Jason Booker—who graduated from UVA— have a son, Jonathan, who is 2. Anne graduated from North Carolina State and is a civil engineer for the Virginia Department of Transportation. They live near Oak Grove.

Jim and Pat Cecil began volunteering with the Cavalier Marching Band when it started in 2003. "I do most anything they need done," he said. "Pat and I feed the band their post-game meal after football games and guard the uniforms while they are eating their pre-game meals."

There are perks to volunteering with the band. "Usually, when they have an away game, they take us with them. When they went to the Gator Bowl, they took us."

'at also volunteers at the University of Virginia hospital in a unit that greets and directs members of families having surgery.

On Fri, Jun 5, 2009 at 11:17 AM, Cecil, James (jgc4d) <igc4d@eservices.virginia.edu> wrote:

Hello Meg,

I have been searching for a website where I might read your article on me, but I have been unsuccessful. It was my understanding it would be in the Thursday, 06/04 edition. Could you help me out on locating it.

Thanks,
Jim Cecil

Meg Hibbert
Editor
Salem Times-Register
and
The New Castle Record

From: Betsy Graves
Sent: Monday, June 15, 2009 3:06 PM
To: Jgc4d@virainia.edu
Subject: Cavalier Daily Article

Dear Mr. Cecil,

Hello! My name is Betsy Graves and I am the Life Senior Associate Editor for the Cavalier Daily, the student-run newspaper at UVa. I saw the article in UVA today about your academic achievements at the University, and wanted to send my congratulations on your recent graduation. I am interested in learning more about your story and would like to write an article about your experiences for our upcoming mail-home "summer edition" of the Cavalier Daily. If you are available, I would love to speak with you sometime at the beginning of this week; please respond to this message or give me a call on my cell (the number is listed below) at your earliest convenience to set up a phone interview. Thanks so much! I look forward to speaking with you soon!

Sincerely,
Betsy Graves

University of Virginia
College of Arts & Sciences 2011
Foreign Affairs A English
540.293.7191

University of Virginia
College of Arts & Sciences 2011
Foreign Affairs & English
540.293.7191

The Roanoke Times

Roanoke.com

Have you heard?—Roanoke.com local Social Security office. Ask for the "Application for Help with Medicare Prescription Drug Plan Costs."

More information about Medicare prescription drug plans and special enrollment periods is available online at www.medicare.goy or by calling (800) 633-4227; or TTY, (877) 486-2048.

CAMPUS

Ashleigh Kingery of Hardy, a law student at Regent University in Virginia Beach, has received a $1,000 national leadership scholarship from Chick-fil-A Inc. The scholarship was awarded to Kingery by Valley View Chick-fil-A operator Bob Childress.

With Ammen, a rising junior at Biyan College, has been elected junior class president for the coming school year. She will lead class officers in planning activities and in representing class interests before the college administration. She is the daughter of David and Elizabeth Ammen of Roanoke.

James Cecil of Palmyra, a Roanoke Valley resident for about 40 years who graduated from Andrew Lewis High School in 1960, has been accepted for membership into Sigma Alpha Lambda. Sigma Alpha Lambda is a national lea4ership and honors organization at the University of Virginia.

Cecil, 65, is an accounts receivable specialist at UVa and is participating in the university's Bachelor of Interdisciplinary Studies program. He is working toward a bachelor's degree in social sciences.

Q&A with James Cedi, one of the oldest UVA Graduates
By Betsy Graves
Cavalier Daily Life Senior Associate Editor

James Cecil recently graduated from the University of Virginia in the class of2009 with a Bachelor of Interdisciplinaiy Studies degree from the School of Continuing and Professional Studies. At the age of 67, he is one of the University's oldest graduates; he started his degree over 30 years ago through taking night classes through a UVa extension center in Roanoke, Virginia and despite working a full-time job and facing various health concerns, recently finished his degree after completing six years of classes on- grounds at the University in Charlottesville. From attending J-term classes to becoming a member of the Alpha Sigma Lambda National Honor Society, Cecil has had a full undergraduate experience. Cecil currently works for the University as an accounts receivable specialist, and shares the story of his journey as a University student here.

When did yon first become interested in the University of Virginia?

"I go back to die forties...I graduated from high school in 1960. Even then I loved the University of Virginia; I followed the athletic teams, had season tickets, and made a few donations [when I could]..." During high school, I raised myself. I wasn't able to go to college like all my friends were, so I went to work and went to school at night. [...] Then I embarked on a career in banking and they wanted me to take bank management classes; so I sort of dropped what I was doing in terms of working towards a degree [to meet those job requirements instead]."

What made you change your mind and pursue a degree through the University?

"I was sitting at home one day and was sort of looking of something else to do….so I went online and looked up job openings at UVA. I applied, went through the interview process, but then there was a hiring freeze—so it didn't work out [After waiting 6–8 months or so], I checked again and found another position. I got the job; then my wife and I moved everything down here [to Charlottesville] so that I could take a position at UVa. […] About a year later, I started thinking and thought it would be neat if I had a degree from UVa. By that time I was about 60 years old…people said, 'what are you going to do with a degree?'" and I said, "I'm going to hang it on the wall and look at it every day." (laughs) "It's sort of like a dream come true to come and work here [at the University]. Even better to be a student here…"

What sort of health challenges did you have to overcome during your studies?

"I had two heart attacks, and then in 2007, one day I collapsed…. (and found out that) I had spine problems [that caused me] to be paralyzed from the waist down. After several months of intensive therapy, I learned to walk again. […] I went from using a wheel chair, to a walker, to a cane, to walking normal. […] Now I'm perfectly normal, except I do suffer with some pain… every day."

What is next for you?

"I got my degree now....and now I'm wondering what I'm going to do with my free time. I used to kid about walking the lawn and retiring at the same time, but (I don't want to do that yet]. I'm enjoying my job too much, and hey, I like being part of the University."

What was it like to be in classes with younger University students?

"It's funny at my age and being married for 35 years…you get in a routine of things. For me to go into class with a lot of younger people and start studying and working again, it sort of rejuvenates and energizes you."

What other things were you involved with during your time as a UVA student?

"My wife and I have been working with the marching band ever since they were first formed—we do whatever needs to be done. We have served food for post-game meals, taken of uniforms…and usually when title band went away for games [like the gator bowl], they took us with them. The kids are so nice, polite, and appreciative as they can be."

How did your wife (who is a retired teacher herself) handle you going back to get a degree?

"She was all for it and has been very good about giving me time to do my homework. […] I think she realized that I had made a lot of sacrifices and (didn't do a lot of things for myself)… and she realized that this was for me."

What is your favorite thing about the University?

"I really think it's hard to say one thing... I like the historic aspect of it I think it's a beautiful—not campus—but grounds. [...] A gentleman once told me, 'Everything you do in life, do it with quality,' and the University does just that."

Can you comment on your overall experience with the BIS program that is offered through the School of Continuing and Professional Studies?

"When I was doing all this, it was no big deal for me; I just signed up for classes, got my grades, and signed up for more classes. [...] Since graduation, I was kind of surprised by the media response [to this accomplishment]; I'm just not used to all this attention. The people that I admire (most) are the people who [went through the program] and have small children and still work full-time—I don't know how they do it [...] For me, it's been quite an experience, and I've never regretted any of it."

FILLING IN WITH ADDITIONAL HISTORY OF MY LIFE

When I first began to write this book, I attempted to cover most of the seventy-seven years I have been alive. Obviously, that was an impossible accomplishment, so I was left with "hitting the highlights." This prevented me from introducing characters such as family members, friends, and acquaintances. I have solved this dilemma by using this chapter to create visions of these characters and how they affected my life.

After this I will cover the chapter titled "Overcoming Illnesses." However, before we head to the emergency room, I will fill in the "gaps" with other adventures and misadventures.

HENRY PRESTON CECIL
01/15/1909–01/18/1972

I have already chronicled that this was my father who abandoned our family when I was in high school. We never knew where he was until fifteen years later. Bill received a phone call one day from an uncle, one of Dad's brothers. He informed us that Dad had died on January 18, 1972. Only then did we learn that when he left us, he moved in to his deceased parents' home in Johnson City, Tennessee, and had lived there ever since. His uncle, also named Jim, told Bill that since he was living alone; no one knew he was dead until two weeks later. A newspaper delivery boy noticed that the newspapers were piling up and alerted the authorities. They entered the house and found his swollen body sitting in a chair in the bathroom. A sad ending to a sad life for a man who had a chance to accomplish great things. What a pity, what a needless waste!

RICHARD BROWDER

I first met Richard in the seventh grade at Broad Street Elementary School in Salem, Virginia. After that, we both attended Andrew Lewis High School where we became close friends. Richard was an outstanding student while maintaining his status as an extremely popular young man. I will always remember one day when it seemed that I had hurt his feelings. I was standing in the hallways, talking to a group of students, when we all laughed at something that I had said. I looked over were Richard stood, and he must have thought we were making fun of him. Our paths did not cross the rest of the day, and I went home feeling guilty. Later at home, regretting what had happened, I decided to walk across the city to his home, which was three miles away. Upon my arrival, we discussed what had happened, and he stated that he did not get that impression at all. I was relieved and glad that I had made the decision to go and talk it over with him, even though I had to hike another three miles back home. We both participated in sports; he was on the track team, and I played football. We mostly had the same friends in high school. His entire family always made me welcome in their home, all except for their cocker spaniel, Pepsi. I have always gotten along with dogs, but he just didn't like me for some reason.

After graduation, Richard went off to attend the University of Virginia (UVA) in Charlottesville, Virginia, and I went to work at Singer Furniture Company in Roanoke, Virginia. However, we managed to stay in touch with each other. On a few occasions I joined him at UVA for some fraternity parties. One night when I got home at midnight after being out on a date, Richard and a friend of his, Jay

Ancarrow, met me at the door. They had been waiting for me to get home so that the three of us could take a trip.

I asked them, "Okay, where are we going?"

Richard replied, "Daytona Beach to the big race."

The race he was referring to was a National Stockcar Racing (NASCAR) event which was the greatest spectacle of the season.

My next question was, "How are we going to get there?"

I was using Bill's car for my date, and mine was parked in the driveway.

"We are going to take your car, of course," he laughed.

My car was a ten-year-old Ford station wagon which cost $325, and back then it would be called a "junker." It was tan in color, and I took the hub caps off and painted the wheels turquoise. It had a coat hanger for a radio antenna and a bicycle reflector pinwheel attached to the front of the hood. It burned more oil than it did gas. Some people asked me if the circus was in town.

Taking all this into consideration I exclaimed, "We will not get out of Virginia in that car."

Jay asked me, "Do you have the title to the car?"

When I replied, "Yes, I have it."

He said, "Bring it with you, if the car breaks down, we will sell it."

I sounded like a good plan, so we threw a mattress in the back, and off we went headed for Daytona Beach, Florida. There were no interstate highways back then, and we would be navigating 660 miles without a map to reach our destination. Our plan was to have a pilot (driver), copilot (codriver), and sleeper in the back. We would take turns at each position. We were cruising along and had reached South Carolina when the fun began. I was taking my turn on the mattress when the car veered to a sudden stop, and there was a loud crashing noise. The other two informed me that a rear wheel bearing had burned out. It was then that Richard informed me that Jay was an engineer and had grown up working on all kinds of cars and trucks. However, there were several problems which needed to be addressed. We were stuck on a lonely highway, and we did not know in which direction lay the nearest town. Also, repairing the wheel bearing required special tools which we did not have and special parts that we also did not have. I became a little concerned when I realized that my Swiss Army knife was not going to be any help. My two "road warriors" started walking south, and I went back to sleep.

As it turned out. they were both extremely lucky and resourceful. They had not walked far when a farmer driving a pickup truck stopped and gave them a ride to a small town, Great Falls, South Carolina. When they arrived in town, it was still early in the morning, and nothing was open yet. They found a pay phone (cell phones had not been invented yet, so you had to use a pay phone in a glass phone booth on a street corner). They looked up the number for the local Ford dealership and found a number for the owner. When they called his home and explained their predicament, he agreed to meet them at the dealership so they could purchase the needed parts. Now they had the parts, but not the device, a wheel puller, that was needed. They also had no transportation back to our car. However, good luck would smile on them again. They ran into the pickup truck driver again, and he offered to give them a ride back. Also, believe it or not, he had the type wheel puller we needed in the back of his truck. We all went to work and in no time were back on the road again. My wife is Catholic, and they believe that St. Christopher is the patron saint of travelers. I would be willing to bet that the name of that pickup truck driver was either Christopher or at least Chris. That is why my two cars have St. Christopher medals.

Next stop, Daytona Beach!

Unfortunately, we were not out of the woods yet. We had just arrived in the outskirts of the city of Daytona Beach where we found a lot of people and businesses. No sooner than we thought we were home free, one of our tires went flat. Of course, we didn't have a spare. We managed to limp a little further before we found a service station. We noticed that they had a pile of old tires lying in the back of the station. We asked the employees what they were going to do with the tires. They, at first, stated that they were to be thrown away, but they decided to sell us one. We worked out a deal with them to pay $5. We did not encounter any more problems while we were at the beach nor on our return trip home. I decided to sell the car about eight months later, and that tire was still on the car. I was able to sell this "wonderful machine" for the same price, $325, that I paid when I bought it originally.

A few months later, Richard called and asked me if I was interested in taking a trip with him.

My first question was, "How are we going to get there?"

He quickly told me, "I will promise you, this trip will not involve an automobile."

I had learned my lesson by this time, so I asked him again, "How are we going to get there?"

He exclaimed, "We are going to hitchhike to Myrtle Beach, South Carolina, only 310 miles."

As it turned out, I went with him, and we not only hitchhiked down there, we hitchhiked back. That is another story for another time. Richard and I have managed to stay in touch although I am living in Charlottesville, Virginia, and he lives in Matthews, Virginia, on the eastern coast. I try to call him about once every couple of weeks. He and his wife, Donna, will always be among my closest friends.

Donnie Butler

One of my good friends, Donnie Butler, was a grade behind me in high school. Donnie, unlike most of my friends, did not go away to college. He instead went to work for a weaving mill in Vinton, a small town in the Roanoke Valley.

During the fifties and the sixties, the culture of young men and women was rock-and-roll music, fast cars, night clubs with live bands, dating, and cruising. The agenda each week was to work at your job or school studies Monday through Friday. Saturday mornings and afternoons were spent preparing for Saturday night. For a guy, one of the most important objectives was being sure your "wheels" (car) was immaculate. This might require washing and waxing every inch of your vehicle. I can only guess what the Saturday routine was for the gals. Unless Donnie and I had a date, we would begin the evening cruising, or we would check out a few hot spots that were "rocking." A lot of our time was also spent working on our cars and attending NASCAR and drag races.

Eventually we both got married, and he had a daughter, Kimberly. After that we didn't get to see each other much. We lost contact with each other when I moved away from Salem. His wife, Susan, recently passed away, and we are trying to stay in touch by phone. My daughter, Anne, lives in Roanoke, and whenever I go visit her, I try to meet him for a breakfast or lunch. I will always cherish his friendship and the "old" days. It sure is fun to remember all the crazy things we did.

(A "Blast from the Past"—hey, let's go hear Perry Caligan and the Royal Kings at the King Club.)

INTRODUCTION TO MY MANY RELATIVES AND FRIENDS

Before introducing some of the people that I have been blessed to know in my life, I want to state my philosophy concerning others. First of all, I have always refrained from judging my fellow men, women, and children. What gives us the right to judge anyone when we, in most cases, do not know what they have experienced in their life? For example, in high school and after graduation, I never discussed my dad. Most of my friends never knew, and if they read this book, I am sure they will be surprised. Even if we know someone well, we probably have little or no knowledge of what they are actually thinking or planning. I have never judged anyone by their skin color, beliefs, appearance, or status. I have always tried to treat them with respect, kindness, and understanding. With that said, I am not a saint, and in many cases I am sure that I could have done more to help many of the people I have met. I also believe that a person should never harbor hatred toward another. I had every reason in the world to hate my father, but instead I chose to put his memory behind me and concentrate on surviving. As it turned out, it was a wise decision.

Jean Holbrook Harding

Jean is another of Pat's teacher friends at William Byrd High School. Later in her teaching career, she was promoted to several Roanoke County administrative positions. Since then she has been staying busy and enjoying retirement. She has always been friendly and caring toward me. It is obvious that she is sincerely concerned about my illnesses and poor health. I appreciate her kind and encouraging words. Jean also has taken it upon herself each year to help organize and implement parties, socials, and reunions for her teacher friends and their spouses. Locating and contacting them after all these years is a daunting task. Some are still in the Roanoke area, but many of them live in other states. It amazes me how many of them drive long distances. It says a lot for the close-knit comradery these teachers have for one another. I hope that Jean will continue to help make it possible for us to meet and greet each other.

Paul and Joy Barnard

I met Paul and Joy through Pat, who taught with them at William Byrd High School. Paul was a physical education teacher, and Joy taught English. Shortly after Paul was hired, he was named the head basketball coach at William Byrd and enjoyed a successful career in that position until he retired. He is still active serving in part-time athletic roles at several other schools. Joy is also enjoying retirement. They have been great friends over the years, and knowing them has enriched our life. We will always cherish the memories of attending sporting events, taking trips together, and especially weeks at Myrtle Beach, South Carolina. The Barnard family includes two daughters, Ginger and Crystal. It is hard to think of them as mature young ladies instead of two cute little girls. They are now grown, married, and have children of their own. If I had to describe the Barnards, I would say they are an example of a "a special all-American family."

AL, SANDY, AND ALMOND ENGLISH

We first met the Englishes when their son, Almond, attended William Byrd High School. Pat was a teacher there, and Anne was a student, so we saw them quite often. The kids graduated and were off to college. Sandy and Al accepted new jobs and moved to Knoxville, Tennessee. We still managed to visit them there when we could. They, like, Pat, loved the beach and decided to move to Pine Knoll Shores, North Carolina. We stayed in touch and spent many vacations visiting them, going on cruises, and enjoying rides on their boat. Sadly, Al passed away recently due to a serious illness. They were a special couple, and now we continue to contact Sandy as often as we can. When we talk to her, she always says the same thing: "Hey, let's hatch a plan."

TOM LAYMAN

I first met Tom when I joined the 2174th Army Reserve Unit. Although we enlisted about the same time, I actually did not know him until after we both had completed our basic training and active duty assignment. As it turned out, we met when we returned home and began our monthly training. After I had graduated from high school, I became an avid tennis player. Tom was also passionate about the sport, and we spent many nights and days playing. At the time he was living in Salem, Virginia, and it was easy to meet each other to play. Unfortunately, he accepted a commercial artist position in Richmond, Virginia. It did not matter since we simply took turns driving back and forth between the two cities. We were fierce competitors, and sometimes our matches lasted for hours at a time. We braved scorching heat, and neither one of us would give up. It got so bad we hoped the other person would win so we could quit.

Tom bought an old pre-revolutionary home in Richmond, and he and his wife completely renovated it using construction charts for structures in Williamsburg. Over the years he is still in Richmond and I am in Charlottesville, but we don't see each other much anymore. Also, we both are retired and not able to play tennis.

Now we only meet occasionally for lunch. He is a great friend whom I miss, even though he beat me like a drum.

CHARLIE SUITER

Another one of my close friends was Charlie, whom I first met in the fifth grade at South Salem Elementary School. In a previous chapter, I mentioned Charlie as the one who persuaded me to go out for football. We remained good friends even after graduating from high school. Charlie attended Virginia Military Institute (VMI) located in Lexington, Virginia. Even though he was highly restricted because of the military requirements of VMI, we tried to see each other when he had some leave time. Also, he was back home in the summer. After he graduated, he was obligated to serve two years in the army and was stationed in South Korea. After he returned from his active duty, Charlie accepted an engineering job on the Gathright Dam in Covington, Virginia. His next job was with the Corps of Engineers on the Virginia eastern coast.

During this period, he met and married a lovely girl, Sylvia, and they moved to Virginia Beach. Unfortunately, after forty-five years of being happily married, she lost a battle with cancer. Charlie still lives in their home, and I have stayed in touch with him by calling him once about every week. I also have visited him for several days three different times. We will always be the closest of friends.

STALEY HESTER AND MALINDA SAYERS

Staley and Malinda were excellent students involved in various clubs and activities at Andrew Lewis High School. They were also two of the most popular pupils in school. Although many of my friends moved away, Staley and Malinda have stayed faithful to their roots and remained in Salem, Virginia. Since I visit my daughter and her family who live in Roanoke quite often, I get to pay them a visit frequently. They will always be my special friends and important part of my life.

MILDRED GARLAND CECIL
6/08/1912–12/17/1987

Our mother was a sweet, fun, loving woman who always enjoyed a good time and a funny joke. She was a kind and considerate person. She tried to protect us and to make our lives pleasant under the worst of situations. The Garland family was huge with a mixture of several brothers and sisters. The roll call went something like this: Bill, Junior, Jack, Rubin, Hazel, and Mildred. When in the long run you added wives, husbands, in-laws, grandchildren, and great-grandchildren, you would have a rather large gaggle.

However, let us concentrate on just my mom with a few short stories. Both Bill and I had newspaper routes when we were little. Since I am not aware if newspaper routes are still in existence, I will explain how they work. The newspaper boy has a bundle of papers delivered to a certain location by a truck, and he either walks or rides his bike to each customer's home on his route. He delivers a newspaper each day, including Sundays. Once a month he collects payment by visiting the customer's home. He then turns the money into the newspaper office and collects his share. It was a good way for a young person to earn a little money and experience their first job.

The first story occurred one Sunday when Bill and I were with our mom. On Sundays the newspapers were always huge and bulky. They were so large you could not deliver them by walking or riding a bike. Therefore, our mom would take us through our routes in her car. We were downtown on Main Street in Salem, and it was about 6:00 AM. The town was quiet, and the streets were empty. We were all in the car as she slowly stopped at a red light. Suddenly the car door flew open and a man with a paper bag jumped in.

He shouted out, "Take me to 438 Academy St." (I do not member the real address; this is a fictional address.)

My mom calmly looked at him and said, "Does this look like a taxicab to you? Get out of my car."

At first, he was so stunned he did not know what to say.

He then took a big breath and meekly stated, "I am sorry, I did not mean to scare you. It is cold out there, and I am freezing. It is not far, and it will only take you a few minutes. It would be so kind of you."

She studied him and then replied, "You will get your ride, but I am warning you that you had better sit still in your seat or you will be back on the curb again."

He sat still as a statue until we let him out, and no one was hurt.

What is strange about this story is that my mom would not normally have acted so cool, calm, and collected. This is evidenced in the next two episodes.

The setting for this tale is a snowstorm on a high bridge. The bridge was on a four-lane street that spanned railroad tracks of two different railroads. It had just begun to snow, and the street was becoming slick. She was driving, and Bill was sitting in the front seat, and I was in the back. We had almost reached the top when the car began to slide backward as we lost traction.

She flew open her door and leaped out, yelling, "Get out, jump, we are all going to die!"

We did not have time to react and just sat there. The car started to slowly turn as it slid back toward the edge. And then... And then...

It gently bumped the curb and stopped. We were all safe and sound and drove home with no further problems.

The next "Mom event" takes the prize, and I have titled it "How to Bag Four Guys."

This setting is the railroad tracks again. The same two railroads, but no bridge. One morning Mom was taking Bill and me to school, and it required driving over the tracks. Most railroad crossings have a gate which comes down when a train approaches. This particular crossing did not have a gate, but instead it had a large round sign which swung back and forth while dinging and blinking. As we approached this crossing, the warning sign came to life and began swinging, flashing, and ringing. Mom correctly pulled the car to the crossing and stopped. We waited, but as we sat there, no train could be seen. Instead a small maintenance vehicle on the tracks approached. These were often seen on the rails, and we called them "dinky cars." Their purpose was to carry four rail maintenance workers. They had wheels which fit on the tracks and were a little larger than a golf cart but much heavier. Two workers stood on each side on small platforms. There were also hand grips mounted on the vehicle.

When they first came in sight, I said to Mom, "Look, Mom, at that little dinky car."

She mumbled something which I did not understand. The next thing I noticed was that she appeared to be lining up the dinky car and the crew with the hood ornament on the front of the car, much like a rifle sight. She then hit the gas when they were directly in the center of the crossing. All I could see out of the front windshield was four guys with fear in their eyes hanging on with one hand as they were becoming airborne. Our car hit the dinky, knocking it off the tracks. We were not hurt and got out to check on the workers. I noticed as Mom approached the four guys, they started backing away. I told her to get in the car and get it off the tracks. Bill and I then apologized, helped them set the dinky back on the rails, and made sure they weren't hurt. I then checked to see if our car had sustained any damage. It had a few small dents and scratches. (Back then cars were made out of metal, not like today's which are mostly rubber and fiberglass.)

These two short stories may sound like I am ridiculing or belittling my mother. I want to state that I would never feel that way about her. She had her moments sometimes and did some "goofy" things. However, she was caught in a life that required protecting her two young children, coping with a drunkard, and basically surviving each day.

After my father left and she was committed to the mental hospital, we tried to visit her often, but it was a long trip for us. She was eventually discharged and returned home. Bill and I were no longer teenagers, and we had plans that did not include staying at home. We lived with Mom for several months, and then we informed her that we wanted to get our own apartments. Bill and I helped her rent a nice place, and we made sure she was called or visited every few days. She adjusted well and seemed to be enjoying life.

Several years passed, and one day about a week before Christmas, I received a phone call at work. It was a gentleman who identified himself as a member of the Salem rescue squad. He informed me that Mom had collapsed while shopping in a clothing store and had been taken to the hospital unconscious.

He told me to go to the hospital and check in at the front desk. I called Bill, told him what had happened, and told him to meet me there.

When we checked in, they directed us to meet a doctor in the chapel. We found the doctor, and he stated that Mom had suffered a massive heart attack and could not be revived. I later learned that she had been shopping in a men's clothing store and was in the process of purchasing a Christmas gift for me.

Our original family of four was back to only two, Bill and me. We were grateful that Mom did not suffer when she passed away. Her final years were happy ones, and I would like to think that her two sons, their wives, and her grandchildren were the reason.

WILLIAM PRESTON CECIL (BILLY, BILL)
05/31/1939–12/06/1991

In previous chapters, I have introduced you to my brother, Bill; however, you got to know him as a young man. Now you will learn about him during the rest of his life after we were left without our parents.

You may be surprised as I was at how the relationship between us turned out. When our mother was admitted to the hospital, we faced the realization that we were going to have to raise ourselves. Since Bill was three years older than me, I accepted him to take on the role of being my new single parent. As it turned out, it did not happen that way at all. Instead, he did not try in any way to serve as an authority over me. Our survival and existence became a joint challenge which required teamwork. It quickly became obvious that because we had no parents, we also had no rules or restrictions. We could go anywhere we wanted to and do anything that pleased us. I am happy and proud to state that neither one of us ever smoked, took drugs, or did anything illegal.

Bill graduated from high school, and I continued by starting my junior year. Even though we had very little money, he was determined to go to college, and he enrolled for the first semester at Virginia Polytech Institute (now VA Tech). At that time, all students were male and had to serve in the corps of cadets.

Due to the fact that our mother was hospitalized and there was no source of income, he dropped out after the first semester to go to work.

For the next two years, he continued to work so we could survive and I could finish high school. Immediately after graduating, it was my turn to go to work. Bill set aside his dream to return to college and continued to work a full-time job. With both of us employed, we began to spend less time together. He had his friends and interests, and I had mine. With that being said, we had some mutual friends, and he involved me with the love of his life. At age nineteen, he helped create the National Railway Historical Society. The Norfolk and Western Railroad owned and operated huge rail facilities in Roanoke. In these shops locomotives were built and repaired and considered to be a vital component of our country's economy. During World War II, Germany considered Roanoke to be a primary target for bombing.

Bill's love of everything involved with railroading bordered on obsession. The most famous locomotive ever built was a product of the Roanoke railyards. It was the fastest and most powerful steam locomotive of its time. It was a J-class engine which Norfolk and Western used to pull passenger trains. The most popular and famous of these passenger trains was named the Powhatan Arrow, and the engine was the 611. This engine was magnificent and beautiful, and its colors were tuscan red with gold trim. Bill owned a van, which was painted identical to this locomotive. His license tags on his van were "NW611."

Several years later, a strange phenomenon concerning the 611 occurred. Bill had gotten married, and his first child, a daughter, Aubie, was born. She was born on June 11, 1974 (611). One year later, my daughter, Anne, was born on June 11, 1975 (611). This becomes a little weirder when recently I was watching an old documentary film concerning the Allied bombing of the German city of Dresden. It was an old German film showing survivors getting on a train. They were entering a rail car with a large number painted on it—"611."

I hope that by "flashing ahead" and telling the story about the J-class 611 locomotive is not confusing. To get us back to a chronological time period (before marriage and babies), I will "flashback" to when both of us were working and getting an opportunity to enjoy life. Bill was busy chasing trains, and I was busy chasing young ladies. To be honest, I am being a little harsh on both of us. It was 1964, and Bill was working hard to make enough to get back to college. I do not remember him dating much, if at all. I had completed my Army active duty, was working a full-time job, a part-time job, and dating as often as I could. Mom was discharged from the mental hospital, and we were united for about a year. We all then decided to separate and get our own apartments. We managed to move close by where we could stay in touch.

Time for another "life changer." Bill was working for a company in Salem, Virginia, Carter Caterpillar. One of his employees, Woody Duncan, asked his sister, Carolyn, if she would like to meet Bill. They met at the annual company Christmas party, and as the saying goes, "the rest is history." She was a student at Madison College in Harrisonburg (now James Madison University) They became involved in a "long-distance" romance that lasted four years. During that time Carolyn continued with her studies and graduated in the spring of 1968. She then accepted a teaching position at William Byrd High School in Vinton, Virginia, a small town next to Roanoke.

While Bill and Carolyn were cultivating their relationship, I was busy in my quest to find my "dream girl." If the truth be known, it was an enjoyable quest. I had a lot of friends, including Carolyn, trying to set me up with blind dates. One of her selections for me was another teacher that taught at William Byrd named Pat Stillwell. When you go on blind dates, you do not know what you are going to get. I had been on plenty of dates that did not fit the description given me by our mutual friend. I remember this evening as one of the worst of my life.

We had decided to go to a movie titled *The Swimmer*. The plot of the movie consisted of a story about a man (Burt Lancaster) who lived in a highly populated suburban neighborhood where everyone had a swimming pool. Burt slowly and methodically dived in each pool until he had swum in everyone. Bill enjoyed it because he had brought a transistor radio and was listening to an Andrew Lewis High School football game (which everyone else in the theater was forced to hear). We topped the evening off with a trip to a pizza parlor. I learned later that Pat hated pizza and could not stand the smell of cheese. It was time to say good night. I normally ended blind dates by saying "I had a good time" or "I enjoyed the evening." Also, I might ask them, "Can I see you again?" This time we both simply said "Good night."

Another two "game changers" occurred in that same fall in 1968. Bill and Carolyn were married, and he reenrolled at Virginia Tech. He already had some credits and managed to graduate in 1970 with a degree in business management. They enjoyed a happy marriage and were blessed with their first child, Auburn (Aubie), on June 11, 1974 (remember the 611). The birth of their second daughter, Rebekah, was in 1980.

It was Bill's misfortune to become diabetic leaving him to battle the onslaught of this terrible disease. There is no cure, and it creates a breakdown of various organs until the patient eventually dies. In December 1981, I had stopped to visit Bill while he was in the hospital. I found him to be in an upbeat, joyful mood. He said to me, "The doctors have told me that I will be discharged tomorrow and that I will be able to go home." I shared this good news with him and then left. The trip from the hospital to our home in Vinton took only about twenty minutes. When I got home, my wife told me Carolyn had called with some bad news. I returned her call, and she informed me that Bill had died of kidney failure. He will be missed forever. He was a wonderful father, husband, and brother.[1]

---

[1] Carolyn had quickly become a widow with two daughters, seven-year-old Aubie and one-year-old Rebekah. Her only income was from her teaching position. I have total admiration for her fortitude, conviction, and resolve. To be a single parent under any situation is a daunting challenge. She alone raised her two children, who developed into model young ladies. They both graduated from college and are now employed in jobs in Washington, DC. Carolyn recently became a proud grandmother of a little boy, Jakob.

WEDDING BELLS AND BABY BUGGIES

The next few chapters are devoted to my wife, my daughter, and my life after marriage. My story about Pat Stillwell, the schoolteacher that I had a "bad" blind date with, was kind of cruel, although I did not intend it to be. If it makes a difference, I want you to know that I ran into her several times after that, and we both laughed about it. She admitted that it was not a pleasant evening and she was not impressed by me. However, as it turned out, we dated off and on for about five years.

During that time she studied at Cambridge in England for a year, so I had no contact with her except for one phone call. I decided to call her one night even though I did not have a number to reach her. Someone told me that if you called the local bobbies' (police) station, they would have her number. I decided to give it a try and was able to reach one of the bobbies.

In a British military voice, he answered, "Sergeant McGregor speaking, how can I be of assistance?"

In my best American voice, I explained, "I am calling from Virginia and trying to reach a friend there named Pat Stillwell."

In a loud voice, he asked, "Where are you calling from?"

My reply was, "VIRGINIA, YOU KNOW, VIRGINIA IN THE UNITED STATES OF AMERICA."

I heard him turn and tell someone else, "Hey, I got some 'bloke' on the phone calling from the colonies."

After he stopped laughing, he gave me the number, and I was able to reach her.

Once Pat returned home, we continued to be friends. It is weird how life sometimes takes strange twists and turns.

For example, it was in 1969 that Pat and I met on our infamous blind date. A lot of changes took place in those five years. We were both not quite ready to settle down. I was changing jobs and moving around, and she was studying in England and traveling. When she returned the pace picked up rapidly. We were seeing each other on a regular basis, and wedding plans were made. We had a wonderful wedding and a romantic tropical honeymoon in St. Thomas. One year later we were blessed with a beautiful baby girl, Anne. We will celebrate our forty-fifth wedding anniversary on June 15, 2019. On June 15, 1974, Ms. Pat Stillwell became Mrs. Pat Cecil, and I became a changed person. They say that opposites attract, and that is true in our case. Pat was a serious, refined professional lady while I was a little crazy and weird. She was the "rudder" that straightened the "course" of my life; it was not a case of me requiring a lot of sharping, but a keener edge was definitely helpful.

Our life together has been a series of ups and downs, as happens in most marriages. It did not take long for a lot of changes to be made. When we returned from our honeymoon, we lived in a small apartment that Pat had been renting. Shortly after that, we moved into a duplex apartment. After moving in, we had to set up a nursery for an addition to the family. Almost exactly one year after our wedding date, a beautiful little girl named Anne Kathryn Cecil was born on June 11, 1975. We stayed in the apartment about three years and then bought our first house. It was in Vinton so Pat could be close to her school. So we moved into our new home with our new baby and settled down to become a normal "all-American family." Pat and I both had good jobs and eventually had another addition to our family, our cat named Taffi.

Pat has two siblings, a younger sister named Marcia and a brother named Michael. Her parents had moved to Martinsville, Virginia, from Buffalo, New York, and that was where the children grew up. Her father, Joe, worked for Dupont and had been transferred to Martinsville. After marrying Pat, I was quickly accepted as a member of the Stillwell family. It eventually became a rather large clan. Her dad, better known as Father, was highly respected, and her mother, Ruth, was one of the kindest and sweetest individuals that I have ever known. I always admired her positive and cheerful attitude toward life. Sadly, both of them are no longer with us.

Marcia and her husband, David, have two children, a son named David Jr. and a daughter named Kathleen. The children are now grown, and both have graduated from college. David Jr. lives in Washington, DC, and Kathleen lives in Charleston, South Carolina. Marcia and David live in Richmond, Virginia, and both are retired.

Mike and his wife, Susan, live in Colorado Springs, Colorado. They have two sons, Brian and Bobby, who have also finished college. Brian is married, and he and his wife, Destiny, are expecting their first child.

A memory we all still cherish was Christmas at the Stillwells'. Even though the three families and their children lived far apart, we all gathered in Martinsville. There were lots of gifts, plenty of food, and family comradery. Just as special was an annual beach vacation for everyone. This celebration was usually held at Hilton Head Island, South Carolina. What made this annual gathering so interesting was seeing how much the kids had grown each year. Fortunately, we have photographs to help preserve the memories.

Pat and I were fortunate to have such a wonderful life. We had a nice home, good jobs, and a magnificent daughter. But time does not stand still and the years have passed much too quickly. Anne was growing up, and before we knew it, she was graduating from high school. She graduated with honors and finished number one in her class. And then it was the time most parents dread—having to leave their son or daughter at college. She chose to attend North Carolina State University in Raleigh, North Carolina. She sighed up for nuclear engineering but later changed her mind.

In 1998, she graduated with honors, earning two degrees in five years. After graduation she took a job offer from an architectural firm in Roanoke. She worked there for a few years and then accepted a position with VDOT (Virginia Department of Highways). She is still employed with them and has been promoted several times to high management positions.

I cannot express how proud I am of Anne and the way she has lived her life. She has excelled in any and all accomplishments she has encountered. I truly believe there are no challenges she could not triumph over. Adding a sparkling personality to all her other attributes results in an amazing persona. The only other thing I have to add is that she is the perfect daughter. She lives in Roanoke, Virginia, with her husband, Jason, and son, Jonathan. I am not much of a poet, but I wrote a poem to honor her on the next page. I was inspired to write this poem one day when I was walking alone on a nature trail. I began my stroll when this beautiful butterfly fluttered beside my face all the way down the path. When I arrived at the end and turned to come back, it stayed with me all the way until the end, where it disappeared.

At the same time Anne graduated from college, 1998, Pat decided to accept an early retirement from teaching. As it turned out, she was about to take on the challenge of being an amateur nurse. It was not so bad since she only had one patient, me.

MY BUTTERFLY

We each have a path of life we travel along the way
Every mile we walk is a year, and every step is a day

At times the trail is smooth and runs down hill
At other times it is rough and tests a person's will

My personal journey has been the best it could be
Mainly because of a wonderful gift that God sent to me

It happened one day miles ago when a lovely butterfly did appear
As I walked along, she fluttered by my side always staying near

We have things in life that give us strength and determination
And from this beautiful creature I found my hope and inspiration

Gracefully she flew on gossamer wings, so fragile yet so strong
And no matter where the path led me, she followed right along

With hues of red, green, and yellow she was a colorful vision
Like multiple rays of bright sunlight passing through a prism

This magnificent creature, this gift from the Lord to me
Has been my faithful companion as I'm sure she'll always be

I know not when my path of life will eventually reach its end
But I know I'll always have my Butterfly, my daughter, my friend

PATRICIA STILLWELL CECIL

I have already stated what a wonderful life Pat and I have enjoyed. I must be honest and confess that at times I have not always been easy to live with. However, she has been understanding over the years, and most of our arguments have been small ones. The greatest challenges and adversities for both of us have been my critical health issues. On the following pages, I have listed many of my "Ongoing Health Issues." These primarily cover the years spanning 2002–2019. The University of Virginia Medical Center has stated that they have records totaling over six hundred pages long on file for me. The other major hospital in Charlottesville, Martha Jefferson Sentara, has another three hundred pages.

I have supplied you with this medical information in the "final chapter," but this particular chapter will concentrate on how my health affected Pat's life. When we moved to Charlottesville in 2002, we left our home in Vinton. We didn't know anyone here and Anne lived a hundred miles away. When I had an emergency of any kind, Pat usually had to call the rescue squad.

Here is a partial list of ACCIDENTS, EMERGENCIES, AND IMMEDI-ATE RISKS:

- HEART ATTACKS—heart attacks can occur anytime and anywhere.
- Pat had to always be on the alert since I have had five. The last one occurred during a church service. I now have to carry a vial of nitroglycerin.
- EMERGENCY ROOM TRIPS—she had to follow behind an ambulance on the way to the hospital countless times.

- EMERGENCY ROOM VISITS—once at the ER, she would have to sit and wait hours until the doctors made their diagnoses.
- BEING ADMITTED TO HOSPITAL ROOM—she would have to spend the night with me unprepared.
- FALLS—due to dizziness and poor stability, I frequently had falls and did not have the strength to get up. In most cases, she would have to call the rescue squad.
- BEING TOTALLY PARALYZED / SPENDING MONTHS IN A WHEEL-CHAIR—pushing a two-hundred-pound man around in a wheelchair is a difficult task for a woman.
- WAITING FOR HOURS DURING RISKY SURGERIES—due to heart issues, all my surgeries were risky.
- THREE DAYS IN A COMA—I had a strep infection in my blood system, and Pat was told that if the source was not found, I would be dead in twelve hours. I remained in a coma for three days.
- VISITS TO ASSISTED-LIVING FACILITIES—I had to live in assisted-living facilities for several months on four different occasions. Pat came to be with me and bring me clean clothes every day.

These are just a few of the challenges that Pat was faced with in trying to make my life at home, in emergency rooms, in hospitals, in assisted living homes, and in rehab centers more tolerable. I asked her what the worst thing was that she had to do. I had a small foot ulcer develop on my left foot. It grew from about an inch to about six inches and took two years to heal. It required a new complicated bandage every day. I was hospitalized for some of the time, but I eventually came home. Once I got home, she had to dress the wound every day. It was a series of wide cloth, which reminded me of how Egyptian mummies were wrapped. I could understand why Pat and nurses hated this chore.

This would be a good opportunity to thank everyone who sent me "get-well" cards and balloons. It also meant a lot to have my family and friends come to see me. Anne was there a lot when I had some kind of a serious procedure. She also brought the rest of her family,

Jason and Johnathan, several other times. David and Marcia Bowles came with David Jr. and Kathleen when I was at the assisted-living facilities and when I was in rehab. Paul and Joy Bernard also came when I was at rehab. Richard Browder and Bobby Blankenbaker came by when I was at an assisted-living home. I want all of you to know that your caring and thoughtfulness was appreciated and helped me greatly in my healing process.

ONLY 24 MORE HOURS TO LIVE?

Several years after I retired from my position at the University of Virginia, Pat and I were dining at a local restaurant on Emmet Street when I became violently ill. After taking me home, she called the rescue squad, and they brought me in to the emergency room. I was not aware of anything after I had left our home since I was in a coma. According to what I was told, I remained in this coma in intensive care for three days. Anne was called in, and she and Pat were told by the head physician, Dr. Andrew Vranic, that I had a streptococcal infection of the blood system (see listed on "My Ongoing Health Issues" list), and if they could not find the source of the infection, I would be dead in twelve to twenty-four hours.

They cut a long incision down each side of my left leg and were able to locate the infection in time.

The first thing that I heard when I came out of my coma was Anne calling my name, and the first thing they heard me say was, "Get these tubes out of me."

HEALTH HISTORY

My medical history began when I was a small boy. Now, it is difficult for me to remember so long ago. However, I have been told that back then, I suffered from several illnesses. According to my parents, I had rheumatic fever and as a result developed a heart murmur. Also, my mother took me to a doctor one day to be treated for mumps. While we were in the waiting room, another young boy was there being treated for the measles. As it turned out, I wound up with the measles and the mumps at the same time.

While growing up after that, my health was great until about forty years ago when I developed type 1 diabetes. As the disease progressed, the medicine dosage increased, and I went from taking one pill a day to becoming an insulin-dependent type 2 diabetic. Other than the diabetes and an occasional cold, my health was almost perfect. In high school, even though I played football, I never suffered a broken bone or any other type of injury.

It was a good thing, because for some reason, I despised hospitals. During one of our football games, a good friend and outstanding player was injured and had been admitted to a local hospital in Roanoke, Virginia. After the game, I went to visit him in hopes of cheering him up. When I got to his room, there was a nurse with him. She asked me to go down the hall to a waiting room for about an hour. When I got there, a young man was pacing back and forth, smoking a cigarette (back then you could smoke in buildings, even hospitals). When I sat down, he stopped walking and stared at me. His clothes were wrinkled, like he had slept in them. However, he had bags under his eyes, which would indicate that he needed rest.

He stared at me and stammered, "Is this your first?"

I had no idea what he was talking about, but he was beginning to get on my nerves. So I decided that I should say something, "Yes, my first all right."

As he lit up another "smoke," his hands were shaking. He blustered out, "I don't know how you do it, I am a nervous wreck. You are calm and collected."

It was about this time that I decided to find somewhere else to wait. I wished him "good luck" and headed out to the hall. The first person I ran into was the nurse who had asked me to wait.

I stopped her and asked, "Is there another room I could wait in? There is a crazy man in the one you sent me to."

She replied, "No, I am sorry. We have an overflow of patients tonight. In fact, that is why we have had to use some rooms on this floor, *the maternity ward.*"

Not until 2005 did any serious health threat materialize. It was my first heart attack. As it turned out, it would be the beginning of a long, dangerous series of health issues.

In order to summarize a list of events which occurred from 2005 to 2018, I have presented a condensed picture.

There were countless rescue squad trips to the emergency room (ER). On one trip I was sitting in the waiting room when a security guard approached me.

He said, "Hello, what do you do here?

I answered, "What do you mean?"

He replied, "Don't you work here? I see you here all the time."

I have had six heart catheterizations and multiple stents, the most recent being five stents in 2017. In conjunction with these surgeries, I had a double bypass and have suffered a total of five heart attacks. During a two-year period, an open ulcer on my right foot refused to heal. It required a fresh bandage each day, and most of my time was spent bedridden. At one point maggots were mailed overnight from a maggot farm in California.

Although it sounds gross, they did a magnificent job of eating all the infection and dead tissue. Another problem that I have encountered on numerous occasions is losing my balance. This has resulted in breaking five ribs and having one concussion.

I, like most people who are diabetic, often suffer from diabetic neuropathy. Diabetic neuropathy is a type of nerve damage that can cause pain and numbness in your legs and feet, problems with your digestive system, urinary tract, blood vessels, and heart. Another problem I have experienced is gout, which is a form of arthritis characterized by severe pain, redness, and tenderness in joints.

ANOTHER DOCTOR STORY

There was another occasion when I was taken to the emergency room due to some heart symptoms. After some preliminary tests in the ER, I was admitted to a hospital room for a week. The head physician came by with his team at the end of the week and stated that they could not determine anything irregular. So they were going to send me home with a dose of medicine. I told him that the rescue squad had picked me up at work and I needed to pick up my car. He assured me it was all right to drive after taking this medicine.

Anne had come down from Roanoke, and she took me by to get my car. The trip from in town to my house is about twenty-five minutes. I got about two miles from our house and blacked out.

In the process I went off the road, mowed down three trees, and turned the car completely around. Anne came up and asked me if I was all right. I told her I was and I thought I could drive the car home. However, when I looked, the whole front end was gone. Of course, even though I was not hurt, they put me in an ambulance and took me back to the hospital. I had the good fortune to see the same doctor who brought a group of interns and nurses with him this time. He told them that I was immortal.

I said, "What!"

He repeated, "Immortal."

I answered, "If that is the case, I am going home and cancel my life insurance."

MY HEALTH SUMMARY

Not listed in any certain order or by date.

- Coronary artery disease.
- Five heart attacks.
- Stents implanted in 2003, 2005, 2008, 2017.
- Erosive esophagitis.
- Essential hypertension.
- Dyslipidemia.
- S/P spinal fusion.
- DDD (degenerative disc disease), lumbar.
- Back pain.
- Atrial tachycardia.
- Obstructive sleep apnea.
- Ventricular ectopic activity.
- Restrictive lung disease.
- Fe-deficiency anemia.
- CMC arthritis.
- Numbness.
- Degeneration of cervical intervertebral disc.
- Cervicalgia.
- Displacement of cervical intervertebral disc without myelopathy.
- Cervical spinal stenosis.
- Limb ischemia.
- Peripheral vascular disease.
- Fracture, metacarpal shaft.
- Other specified diabetes mellitus with foot ulcer.

- Carpal tunnel syndrome of right wrist.
- Coronary artery disease involving bypass graft of native heart without angina pectoris.
- Several fall from ground level.
- Multiple fractures of five ribs of left side.
- Streptococcal infection.
- Hyperkalemia.
- Right heart failure.
- Vancomycin-resistant enterococci infection.
- Left knee pain.
- Leg pain.
- Hip fracture requiring operative replacement of left hip.
- H/O osteomyelitis.
- Acute post-operative pain.
- Blurry vision, bilateral.
- Right knee pain.
- S/P total hip arthroplasty.
- MRSA infection.
- Knee effusion, left.
- Pain in right finger.
- Leukocytosis.
- Atherosclerosis of coronary artery-s/p CABG.
- Diabetic peripheral neuropathy (HCC)
- Peripheral neuropathy, idiopathic.
- Peripheral vascular disease.
- Diabetic polyneuropathy.
- Edema.
- Paroxysmal A-Fib-s/p ablation.
- Severe kidney disease (stage 4).
- Sinus bradycardia.
- Type 2 diabetes (insulin dependent).
- GERD (gastroesophageal reflux disease).
- First-degree AV block.
- Anemia.
- Cervical spinal stenosis.
- Congestive heart failure.

- Esophageal ulceration.
- Hypertension.
- Nephrolithiasis.
- Osteomyelitis of left foot.
- S/P spinal fusion.
- Benign essential hypertension.
- Cardiac catheterization performed with a 90 percent in stent restenosis of the mid-RCA treated with a Taxus stent.
- Constant nausea and vomiting over a period of several months, loss of appetite, and dangerous weight reduction.
- Open wounds/ulcerations
- Wound debridement.
- High risk for loss of limbs.
- Nonhealing wounds.
- Due to new risks and complications, it was determined that there was a possibility of staged surgical debridements, amputation of foot, amputation of lower extremity/leg, chronic pain, swelling, and disability.
- Surgery on left foot to salvage limb performed.
- Several weeks of physical training rehabilitation.
- Displaced oblique fracture through the diaphysis of the diaphysis of the right hand.

MY ONGOING HEALTH ISSUES

The following is a list of my ongoing health issues according to medical records furnished by University of Virginia Medical Center and Martha Jefferson Hospital in Charlottesville, Virginia:

- Amputation—my left toe became infected and had to be amputated.
- Acute postoperative pain—chronic pain in response to surgery.
- Atrial tachycardia—a type of heart rhythm problem in which the heart's electrical impulse comes from ectopic pacemaker in the upper chambers of the heart, rather than from the sinoatrial node.
- Atrial fibrillation—an abnormal rapid and irregular heart rhythm which increases risk of heart failure, dementia, and stroke.
- Blurry vision, bilateral—macular degeneration, loss of central vision, blurred vision and distorted vision.
- Carpal tunnel syndrome—a common condition that causes pain, numbness and tingling in the hands and arms.
- Cervical spinal stenosis—degenerative changes in the spine that cause the spinal canal to narrow, causing numbness, tingling, weakness or pain in the hands, arms, and legs.
- Cervicalgia—intense pain in neck and shoulder similar to an electric shock from the neck to the arms.

- Chronic back pain—causing shooting or piercing pain in the lumbar area.
- CMC arthritis—arthritis of the thumb joint, causing stiffness and pain.
- Collagen vascular disease—term used to describe systemic autoimmune diseases such as rheumatoid arthritis, systemic lupus erythematosus, and systemic sclerosis.
- Congestive heart failure—congestive heart failure occurs when your heart muscle does not pump blood as well as it should. Narrowed arteries or high blood pressure gradually leave your heart too weak or stiff to fill and pump efficiently.
- Coronary artery disease / coronary bypass grafting—disease causes arteries to become blocked, thus cutting off blood flow leading to a heart attack; bypass surgery enables the surgeon to bypass the clogged artery and open up one which is clear.
- DDD—degenerative disc disease refers to symptoms of back and neck pain caused by wear and tear on a spinal disc.
- Degeneration of cervical intervertebral disc—symptoms are a neck pain and stiff neck, causing pressure on nerves running through the spinal cord which can result in pain, numbness, or weakness radiating down your shoulder, arm, and hand.
- Diabetes mellitus type one—a chronic condition in which the pancreas produces little or no insulin. The patient injects insulin once or several times a day or has it injected by an automatic pump. There is no cure for diabetes.
- Diabetic neuropathy—neuropathic pain, or nerve pain, is one of the most intense types of pain, often described as sharp, stinging, or burning.
- Displacement of cervical intervertebral disc without myelopathy—refers to protrusion or herniation of the disc between two adjacent bones (vertebrae) of the cervical spine in the neck (vertebrae C2 through C7).

- Dyslipidemia—an abnormal amount of blood lipids.
- Dyspnea—the feeling that you can't catch your breath or get enough air in your lungs. Other symptoms may be breathless, tightness in chest, or inability to breathe deeply.
- Erosive esophagitis—inflammation, irritation, or swelling of the lining of the esophagitis, the tube that runs from the throat to the stomach. This may cause difficulty swallowing, pain when swallowing, burning sensation, acid reflux and bleeding.
- Essential hypertension—high blood pressure which does not have a known secondary cause. It is also known as primary hypertension. Blood pressure is the force of blood against your artery walls as your heart pumps blood through your body.
- Frequent falls due to dizziness and lack of balance—at least twelve have occurred; one resulted in five broken ribs and another one a concussion.
- Fall in doctor's office—I fell in a doctor's office and did not feel like I needed any medical attention. A week later, a CT scan showed I had a concussion.
- Fe-deficiency anemia—too few healthy red blood cells due to too little iron in the body.
- Finger pain—both right and left hands and fingers developed numbness, weakness, cramps, and pain.
- Flexor tendinitis—flexor tendons are the tissues that control movement in your hand; a flexor injury can make it impossible to bend your fingers or thumb.
- Fracture-metacarpal shaft—fractures of the metacarpal shaft are usually the result of direct or indirect trauma.
- Gerd (gastroesophageal reflux disease)—Gerd happens when a muscle at the end of your esophagus does not close properly. This allows stomach contents to leak back, or reflux, into the esophagus.
- GI bleeding (gastrointestinal bleeding), also known as gastrointestinal hemorrhage—all forms of bleeding in the gastrointestinal tract, from the mouth to the rectum.

- Herpes zoster (shingles)—this is an outbreak of a rash or blisters on the skin caused by the varicella-zoster virus. A rash of fluid filled blisters create severe burning pain.
- H/O osteomyelitis—osteomyelitis is the medical term for a bone infection. Bone infections are caused when a break in the skin allows germs, usually bacteria, to spread into bone tissue.
- HTN (hypertension)—HTN is a medical term for high blood pressure. Uncontrolled high blood can increase risks of serious health problems, including heart attack and stroke.
- Hyperkalemia—this is an a potently life-threating metabolic problem caused by inability of the kidneys to excrete potassium, impairment of the mechanisms that move potassium from the circulation into the cells, or a combination of these factors.
- Infected foot ulcer—a wound that becomes infected and can result in amputation. In my case, I developed a wound to my heel, which took two years to heal.
- Left knee pain—pain in and around the knee that may indicate a condition affecting the knee joint itself or the soft tissue around the knee.
- Knee effusion—swelling of the knee occurs when excess synovial fluid accumulates in or around the knee joint.
- Leg pain—leg pain can be traced to problems in your lower spine. It can also be caused by blood clots, varicose veins, or poor circulation.
- Leukocytosis—leukocytosis refers to an elevation in the total white blood cell count (WBC). It is most often caused by infections, hypoxic tissue damage, trauma, inflammatory diseases, or malignancy.
- Limb ischemia—limb ischemia is a severe blockage in the arteries of the lower extremities, which markedly reduces blood flow.
- MRSA infection—methicillin-resistant staphylococcus aureus (MRSA) is a bacterium that causes infections in dif-

ferent parts of the body. It is tough to treat because of its resistance to commonly used antibiotics.

- Neuromuscular disorder—neuromuscular junction disorders result from the destruction, malfunction, or absence of one or more key proteins involved in the transmission of signals between muscles and nerves.
- NSTEMI (non-ST-elevation myocardial infraction)—a myocardial infraction is a medical term for a heart attack.
- OSA (obstructive sleep apnea)—hypopnea is a sleep disorder that involves cessation or significant decrease in airflow in the presence of the breathing effort.
- Peripheral vascular disease—a blood circulation disorder that causes the blood vessels outside your heart and brain to narrow, block, or spasm.
- Restrictive lung disease (also known as restrictive ventilatory defects)—are a category of extrapulmonary, pleural, or parenchymal respiratory diseases that restrict lung expansion, resulting in a decreased lung volume, an increased work of breathing, inadequate ventilation, and oxygenation.
- Radiculopathy (also known as "pinched nerve")—a set of conditions where one or more nerves are affected and fail to work properly. This can result in pain, weakness, numbness, or difficulty controlling specific muscles.
- Severe chronic kidney disease—also called kidney failure, results in the loss of kidney function. Your kidneys filter wastes and excess fluids from your blood, which are then excreted in your urine.
- S/P spinal fusion—spinal fusion is a surgical procedure used to correct problems with the small bones in the spine (vertebrae). It is essentially a "welding" process. The basic idea is to fuse together two or more vertebrae so they heal into a single, solid bone.
- S/P total hip replacement—a total hip replacement (also called total hip arthroplasty); the damaged bone and cartilage is removed and replaced with prosthetic components.

- Streptococcal infection of blood system—if bacteria get into parts of the body where it is not usually found, like blood, muscle, and the lungs, the results can be devastating, even fatal. I was in intensive care in a coma. My wife, Pat, was advised by the doctors that I only had twelve to twenty-four hours to live if the infection was not found.
- Unstable angina—unstable angina is a condition in which your heart doesn't get enough blood flow and oxygen and can lead to a heart attack.
- Ventricular ectopic activity—an ectopic rhythm is an irregular heart rhythm due to a premature heartbeat. It is also known as premature atrial contraction, premature ventricular contraction, and extrasystole.

SURGICAL HISTORY

- Adenoidectomy—the surgical removal of the adenoid for reasons which include impaired breathing through the nose, chronic infections, or recurrent earaches.
- Amputation of one toe—removal of toe due to infection.
- CABG—coronary artery double bypass open-heart surgery.
- Cardiac catheterization—a procedure used to detect the presence of disease in the coronary arteries, the heart muscle, the valves within the heart.
- Carpal tunnel release—surgery in which the transverse carpal ligament is cut, which releases pressure on the median nerve in the hand.
- Diskectomy—spinal surgery which requires full or partial removal of the back portion of a vertebra.
- Hip replacement—entire replacement of broken hip.
- Lithotripsy—destruction of kidney stones using shock waves.
- Meta carpel bone fraction—an injury, usually to a broken hand, which may require operative intervention.
- Placement of loop recorder in chest—implant of recording device which is used to monitor irregular heartbeat.
- Removing of plaque in arteries—by inserting a tiny tube in the arteries, plaque can be sucked out or broken up.
- Thoracic diskectomy—the removal of a disc in your spine located in the middle back area from your shoulder blades to just under your rib cage.
- Benign essential hypertension

- Cardiac catheterization performed with a 90 percent in stent restenosis of the mid-RCA treated with a Taxus stent.
- Constant nausea and vomiting over a period of several months, loss of appetite, and dangerous weight reduction.
- Open wounds/ulcerations.
- Wound debridement.
- High risk for loss of limbs.
- Nonhealing wounds.
- Due to new risks and complications, it was determined that there was a possibility of staged surgical debridements, amputation of foot, amputation of lower extremity/leg, chronic pain, swelling, and disability.
- Surgery on left foot to salvage limb performed.
- Several weeks of physical training rehabilitation.
- Displaced oblique fracture through the diaphysis of the diaphysis of the right hand.

MEDICAL ACKNOWLEDGMENTS

The following acknowledgments are for the highly skilled medical professionals who have treated me and kept me alive for the past seventeen years. They excel in not only their medical expertise but also in their personal relationships with their patients:

Dr. James Browne, Orthopedics
Dr. Sandhya Chhabra, Endocrinology
Dr. Andrew Collins, Ophthalmology
Dr. Angelo Dacus, Orthopedics
Dr. Hakan Dagli, Family Medicine
Dr. Kevin McConnell, Nephrology
Dr. Christopher Rembold, Cardiovascular Medicine
Dr. Francis Shen, Orthopedic Surgery
Dr. Andrew Vranic, Internal Medicine
Abbie Harrell, RN
Elizabeth Gochenour, RN
Leigh Kloss, RN, BSN
Richard Schneider, Certified Wound Nurse

Some Other Acknowledgments

Mark O'Connell

It always amazes me what a small world it is and how people move in so many directions only to meet again. Mark first saw me as a small boy in Salem, Virginia. I don't know where his travels took him, but as you know, mine went from Salem to Roanoke to Christiansburg to South Boston to Radford to Roanoke to Vinton to Charlottesville, and when I meant him, he was living in Green County.

He has been a great friend and mentor. It has helped so much to be able to pick his brain concerning the fine art of being an excellent author. If you haven't read his book, *The Team the Titans Remember*, I highly recommend it (and it has my picture in it). Seriously, he has been a true friend, and I can only hope to repay him in some way.

Matt and Becky Marshall

Matt and Becky have been our friends for a long time. I first met Becky when she worked in her BIS (bachelor of interdisciplinary studies). She and Matt have always been so kind and thoughtful when I had health issues. She recently helped me a lot with my computer and my typing since I had little or no use of my right hand. Even though they have had health problems of their own, they take time to help us in so many ways.

Donna Plasket and Kathryn Buzzoni

Both Donna and Kathryn worked in the BIS office when I was a student. They made my transition through the academic journey a pleasant and exciting adventure. Donna was the director then but retired in 2014. I guess she heard that I had also retired.

Kathryn is now serving as an academic partnership program director. I mentioned earlier that she was the one who signed me up for classes. Over the years, we also became good friends, and I saw her often when some of my classes were in the same building as her office.

My Current Health at This Time

In the last eight chapters, I have tried to chronicle my medical history, beginning approximately seventeen years ago. During that period of time, I have suffered a multitude of diseases, accidents, and illnesses. Some of these ailments have been minor while others have been life threatening. Fortunately, I have been blessed with expert care by rescue squad personnel, physicians, and nurses. Also, my family and friends have given me support, which has enabled me to persevere and to survive. The end result is that I am now cured and free of most of the suffering. For this reason, I would like to report my present health.

These are the Two Issues: Spinal Degeneration and Heart Attacks

Degeneration of Cervical Intervertebral Symptoms are a neck pain and stiff neck, causing pressure on nerves running through the spinal cord, which can result in pain, numbness, or weakness, radiating down shoulders arm and hand. Displacement of cervical intervertebral disc without myelopathy refers to protrusion or herniation of the disc between two adjacent bones of the cervical spine in the neck. This is a result of the degeneration of my spinal cord in 2006, which left me totally paralyzed below the waist. I have had a second operation since then, but I live with severe pain every day. The pain travels either in my right hand, my right forearm, my right or left shoulder, or both sides of my neck. If I stand in one place for more than a few minutes or I walk a short distance, I experience excruciating pain in my lower back. My spinal surgeon is aware of this, but additional surgery is not an option due to the high risks of a heart attack.

As I have previously reported, I have suffered five heart attacks. In addition to those, I have had several scares with atrial fibrillation (AF). This is an abnormal rapid and irregular heart rhythm, which increases risk of heart failure, dementia, and stroke. Also, I have had a CABG, which is a coronary artery double bypass open heart surgery. There is not a whole lot I can do to prevent a heart attack, except trying to recognize the symptoms. I do carry around a vial of nitroglycerin in case there is an attack.

So there is a capsule summary of my current health. I try to block out the pain and take each day as it comes. There is always tomorrow to look forward to.

The Final Page

Yes, this is the final curtain—at least for this book. I am sure it will be some time before this "best seller" hits the shelves, but according to my calendar, today is March 29, 2019. Be sure you take note of the year, because it may not make it this year. In fact, all my friends and some of my enemies may get a copy for Christmas.

Let us change the subject. Last week, on Thursday, March 21, 2019, I had my seventy-seventh birthday, and it was something. Normally my daughter Anne and her family come down from Roanoke to join Pat and me for a nice steak dinner. However, it was in the middle of the week, and they could not make the trip. So we decided to eat alone, which was all right. I was looking forward to some nice gifts, but none appeared. Pat said that a tiny pocketknife that I had ordered from Amazon was one of my gifts, and a pair of Bermuda shorts that didn't fit was the other. It was a cold day, and it poured rain, so we stayed home and shared a bowl of tomato soup. There was no birthday cake, and we found out that a lit candle does not float in a bowl of soup. Seriously, I felt very blessed that I had managed to live seventy-seven years. The only thing that I will ever feel like I have missed is the opportunity to do more for others.

Well, here I sit, trying to figure out how to wrap this thing up. It has been fun, and I hope you have been entertained by my little tales. You may not believe it, but for every story in this book, I have at least two or three more that I can tell. Of course, many of them must be kept locked away in my chest of secrets to never be known.

My hope is that by reading this book, you will gain inspiration to overcome any adversity you encounter in your lives.

ABOUT THE AUTHOR

Jim Cecil was born in Johnson City, Tennessee, and currently resides at Lake Monticello, which is in Fluvanna County, near Charlottesville, Virginia, with his wife, Pat. Growing up he enjoyed playing tennis and golf. Jim is also a collector of die-cast models of World War II fighter planes. Now retired from the University of Virginia, he spends his time reading, listening to music, and solving crossword puzzles.

CPSIA information can be obtained
at www.ICGtesting.com
Printed in the USA
BVHW070937110220
572026BV00005B/525